Sweet Sue

Sweet Sue

A PLAY IN TWO ACTS
BY
A. R. Gurney, Jr.

Nelson Doubleday, Inc.
Garden City, New York

For Nikos Psacharopoulos

The world premiere of *Sweet Sue* was presented by the Williamstown Theatre Festival, Nikos Psacharopoulos, Artistic Director.

Originally produced on Broadway by Arthur Whitelaw, Richard Button, and Byron Goldman, *Sweet Sue* opened at the Music Box Theatre on January 8, 1987 with the following cast:

SUSAN	Mary Tyler Moore
SUSAN TOO	Lynn Redgrave
JAKE	John K. Linton
JAKE TOO	Barry Tubb

The production was directed by John Tillinger. The scenery was by Santo Loquasto, costumes by Jess Goldstein, lighting by Kenn Billington, creative photography by FPG International, New York and background display by Kodak Duratrans. The production stage manager was Ed Aldridge.

CHARACTERS AND SCENE

SUSAN WEATHERILL: a woman in her late forties, to be played by two actresses—Susan and Susan Too.

JAKE: a man in his early twenties, to be played by two actors—Jake and Jake Too.

The play takes place primarily in the third-floor studio of Susan's house in a suburb outside New York during the course of a recent summer.

NOTES

On the Casting:
This is a two-character play to be performed by four actors. The lines and scenes are distributed so that no actor or actress dominates the play. It would be a mistake to break the parts down into different psychological aspects or alter egos of the characters. Rather we should see two different but complete approaches to each role, as if we were attempting to sketch the human figure from two different perspectives.

On the set:
Similarly, the set should reflect this sense of sketching. Upstage, there should be shelves containing many of the props used in the play. Behind them, the suggestion of a window and a vision of suburban greenery. Clothes trees may also hold costumes and accessories. Chairs, stools, and a cot are distributed informally around, and are introduced into a scene by the actors as they are needed. There is a loveseat downright. Downstage left is a large table which can be converted into a drawing table, a kitchen counter, or a dinner table as necessary. The overall effect is that of an artist's studio, within which other spaces can emerge.

On the staging:
Scenes should overlap when possible, even as an artist's sketches might present several perspectives or positions simultaneously. It is as if we were leafing through a sketchbook, retaining an image of one drawing even as we move onto the next.

Act One

ACT ONE

(At rise: The lights come up on SUSAN, *sketching* JAKE, *who sits naked, his back to the audience, downstage on a stool. Upstage,* SUSAN TOO *stands by the daybed, watching* JAKE TOO *stuff clothes into a backpack. Both* SUSANS *wear jeans with shirts or smocks)*

SUSAN: *(As she sketches)* This is the way it should have ended, Jake.

JAKE: You think so?

SUSAN: Absolutely. It would have solved everything.

JAKE: Maybe you're right, Mrs. Weatherill.

SUSAN: And you would have called me Susan.

JAKE: Susan . . .

SUSAN: See how easy that is? Because now we have a professional relationship, Jake.

JAKE: Right, Susan.

SUSAN: I'll draw a beautiful picture and then you'll put on your pants and go home.

*(*SUSAN TOO *turns from the window)*

SUSAN TOO: You're dreaming again.

SUSAN: I know . . .

SUSAN TOO: The same dumb old dream . . .

SUSAN: Got a better one?

SUSAN TOO: How about a short, sweet, civilized good-bye? *(She turns to* JAKE TOO) It's better this way, Jake.

JAKE TOO: *(Packing)* You think so?

SUSAN TOO: Oh yes. I think it's definitely for the best.

JAKE TOO: Maybe you're right, Mrs. Weatherill.

SUSAN TOO: At least you could call me Susan as you go.

JAKE TOO: Susan . . .

SUSAN TOO: I mean, we've known each other since June.

JAKE TOO: Right.

(He hoists his backpack to his shoulder)

SUSAN TOO: Well, then, good-bye, Jake.

(She holds out her hand)

JAKE TOO: Good-bye, Susan.

(They shake hands)

SUSAN: *(From her stool, watching)* Is that *it?*

SUSAN TOO: I thought so. Yes.

SUSAN: Just shaking *hands?*

SUSAN TOO: *(Quickly)* I think I could survive a good-bye kiss, Jake.

JAKE TOO: *(Kissing her affectionately)* Good-bye, Mrs. Weatherill—I mean, good-bye, Susan.

(JAKE TOO starts off)

SUSAN: And you'd let him go? Just like that?

SUSAN TOO: Certainly.

SUSAN: I don't believe it.

SUSAN TOO: *(Quickly)* Jake!

(JAKE TOO *stops)*

SUSAN: Knew it.

SUSAN TOO: *(To* JAKE TOO) How about a beer before you go?

JAKE TOO: O.K.

SUSAN TOO: We'll sit down, you and I, and have a beer.

JAKE TOO: O.K.

(He takes off his backpack)

SUSAN: *(To* SUSAN TOO) You don't like beer.

SUSAN TOO: I do. I love it. Occasionally. *(Takes* JAKE TOO'*s arm)* Come on. We'll see if we can find a good, cold beer.

(They start off)

SUSAN: *(Calling after* SUSAN TOO) You hate beer and you know it.

SUSAN TOO: Why don't you stick to your professional relationship?

(SUSAN TOO *and* JAKE TOO *go off up right.* SUSAN *returns to sketching* JAKE)

SUSAN: Getting bored? Just sitting there?

JAKE: Actually, I'm psyched.

SUSAN: Well, all I know, Jake, is that for twenty-five years, ever since art school, I've had to work from photographs—copying, illustrating, regurgitating—until I thought I'd totally lost track of the human form.

JAKE: And then you discovered mine.

SUSAN: Exactly! What a pleasure this is! To work from nature. To look at life directly.

JAKE: It's a pleasure for me, too.

SUSAN: Really? You mean that?

JAKE: Sure. How many guys in the world get paid twenty-five bucks an hour to sit around naked in front of a great-looking woman?

SUSAN: Thank you, Jake.

JAKE: You're welcome, Mrs. Weatherill.

SUSAN: *Who*, for God's sake?

JAKE: I mean, Susan.

(SUSAN TOO *returns with a can of beer, followed by* JAKE TOO, *also with a beer)*

SUSAN TOO: He'd never do that.

SUSAN: Why not?

SUSAN TOO: Because he kept saying he wouldn't. You'd be lucky to get him in a towel.

(JAKE *now covers himself with a towel)*

JAKE: Actually, this feels a little easier, Mrs. Weatherill.

SUSAN TOO: See?

SUSAN: *(To* SUSAN TOO) Thanks a bunch.

(She returns to her sketching)

SUSAN TOO: *(To* JAKE TOO*)* I thought we'd sit here.

JAKE TOO: O.K.

(He sits on the loveseat)

SUSAN TOO: We'll make this a Jewish good-bye, Jake. Do you know what that is?

JAKE TOO: Not really.

SUSAN TOO: Well, you see, the Wasps leave without saying good-bye. The Jews say good-bye without leaving.

JAKE TOO: That's a good one, Susan.

SUSAN: *(Looking up from her sketching)* That's an old one, Susan.

SUSAN TOO: *(Joining* JAKE TOO *on the loveseat)* Let's talk about music, Jake.

JAKE TOO: Music?

SUSAN TOO: The great equalizer.

JAKE TOO: Oh, I don't know. I took a course this spring at Dartmouth and the professor said that never before in history has there been such a tragic gap between the generations.

SUSAN TOO: Tragic gap?

JAKE TOO: And this gap is demonstrated by our different tastes in music.

SUSAN TOO: Oh, but surely there's music to bridge that gap.

JAKE TOO: He didn't mention any.

SUSAN TOO: How about Mozart? How about Puccini? *(Ironically)* How about a song named "Sweet Sue"?

JAKE TOO: It must have slipped his mind.

SUSAN TOO: What? He forgot my theme song? I'll have to send him one of my greeting cards: "Lovingly designed by Sweet Sue."

SUSAN: *(Singing as she sketches)* "Every star above . . . Knows the one I love . . ."

SUSAN TOO: *(Singing)* "Sweet Sue . . . Just you . . ." Didn't you ever hear that song before this summer?

JAKE TOO: I might have.

SUSAN TOO: You must have.

JAKE TOO: I think maybe they play it in airports and bus stations.

SUSAN: *(Still sketching)* So much for music.

SUSAN TOO: Well, I don't see you accomplishing very much in the art department.

SUSAN: I've never been very good at drawing towels.

JAKE: *(Starting to get up)* Maybe I'd better go.

SUSAN: No, please! No.

SUSAN TOO: *(Coming down to JAKE)* At least finish my beer.

(She hands him her beer)

JAKE: Hey, thanks.

SUSAN TOO: *(To SUSAN)* You can put it in the drawing. Call it *Boy with Beer.*

SUSAN: Or how about *Man with Can?*

JAKE: I like that better, Mrs. Weatherill.

BOTH SUSANS: Who?

JAKE: *(Toasting them with his beer)* I like that better, Susan.

(JAKE TOO *picks up his backpack)*

JAKE TOO: I'll be going then.

SUSAN: *(Getting up)* Wait! I never finished my drawing.

JAKE TOO: Maybe it's just as well.

SUSAN: I don't even have a snapshot I can copy.

JAKE TOO: I'll send you one this fall.

SUSAN: You won't.

SUSAN TOO: You never will.

SUSAN: After you've gone, I'll have nothing.

SUSAN TOO: At least I have this.

(SUSAN TOO *takes the drawing pad and pencil from her)*

SUSAN: *(To JAKE TOO)* I'll drive you to the bus then.

JAKE TOO: That's O.K.

SUSAN: I want to drive you.

JAKE TOO: I don't want you to.

SUSAN: Have you got another ride?

JAKE TOO: Maybe.

SUSAN: With that girl?

JAKE TOO: Maybe.

(He is almost out)

SUSAN: *(Anguished)* Jake! *(He stops and turns)* I have my pills, Jake. Remember my pills. *(She takes them from her shirt pocket)* I might take them. I might take the whole bottle!

JAKE TOO: Not you, Mrs. Weatherill. You're too big for that.

(He goes out. SUSAN stands looking after him, holding the pills)

JAKE: *(Finishing the beer, getting up from the stool)* I'll be going then.

SUSAN TOO: Wait! I never finished my drawing.

JAKE: Maybe it's just as well.

SUSAN TOO: I don't even have a snapshot I can copy.

JAKE: I'll send you one this fall.

SUSAN: *(At window, looking out)* He's gone.

SUSAN TOO: *(To JAKE)* At least listen to some music first.

JAKE: What kind?

SUSAN TOO: I'll find something. *(To SUSAN)* Give me a hand here!

SUSAN: *(Turning to her)* He's gone forever.

SUSAN TOO: Not yet. Quickly. Take over while I find some music. *(Hands her the drawing pad)*

SUSAN: I can't.

SUSAN TOO: Please. Help me hold him. (SUSAN *takes the drawing pad and sits downstage center.* SUSAN TOO *crosses to a stack of records on one of the shelves)* I've got some great operas here, Jake.

JAKE: Operas?

SUSAN: He likes the Talking Heads, not *Tosca*.

SUSAN TOO: *(Shuffling through records)* You like *Tosca*, don't you, Jake? Everyone likes *Tosca*.

JAKE: I don't know *Tosca*.

SUSAN: *(Trying to sketch him as he stands)* Don't move . . . Hold still.

SUSAN TOO: How about this? *(She puts a record on)* I was listening to this the day you arrived.

(The music comes up: the aria "Visi d'arte" from Tosca*)*

SUSAN: This brought you in, Jake. This landed you on my doorstep, with that dumb backpack and those flowers sticking out.

*(*JAKE TOO *enters upstage, as described)*

SUSAN TOO: Listen. She's singing about how she lives for art, lives for love . . .

JAKE: Sorry, Mrs. Weatherill.

(He starts to leave again)

SUSAN: Oh, just listen, Jake, please. Let's go back. Let's start again from square one.

JAKE: 'Bye, Mrs. Weatherill.

(He goes out as JAKE TOO *comes downstage)*

JAKE TOO: *(Simultaneously with* JAKE*'s exit line)* Hi, Mrs. Weatherill. (BOTH SUSANS *jump, turn to look at him)* Jesus. Did I scare you? I kept calling. First at the door, then all the way up the stairs.

SUSAN TOO: The music might be a little loud.

JAKE TOO: I thought I'd follow it to its source.

SUSAN: I'll turn it off.

(SUSAN *goes to turn the music off*)

JAKE TOO: I'm Jake.

SUSAN TOO: Who?

(She looks at SUSAN*)*

SUSAN: Ted's roommate.

SUSAN TOO: Ah.

JAKE TOO: We met up at Dartmouth last fall? Parents' weekend?

SUSAN TOO: Of course!

JAKE TOO: You took Ted and me out to dinner at the Surf and Turf.

SUSAN: It all comes back.

SUSAN TOO: I remember very well, Jake.

JAKE TOO: Good to see you again, Mrs. Weatherill.

SUSAN: Good to see you too, Jake.

JAKE TOO: *(Awkwardly handing her the flowers)* Oh. These are for you.
I got them at the bus station.

SUSAN: Why, thank you.

(She takes them)

JAKE TOO: It's a pretty trivial house present from someone who'll be staying all summer.

SUSAN TOO: All summer?

SUSAN: All summer *long?*

JAKE TOO: Didn't Ted tell you?

SUSAN: No, actually.

JAKE TOO: Jesus! He said it was O.K. He said he'd lined up two houses to paint and I could stay right here while we were doing it.

SUSAN TOO: Well, he forgot to tell me.

SUSAN: Let's take care of these.

(She takes the flowers across to the drawing table, gets a vase from the shelf)

SUSAN TOO: They're lovely, by the way. I love them.

JAKE TOO: God, maybe I should turn around and grab the next bus back to Ohio.

BOTH SUSANS: No!

SUSAN: Of course you can stay, Jake.

SUSAN TOO: *(Low, to* SUSAN*)* But not all summer.

SUSAN: *(Low, to* SUSAN TOO*)* But Ted said he could.

SUSAN TOO: *(Low, to* SUSAN*)* I mean, what are we? A hotel? A summer *camp?*

SUSAN: *(Low, to* SUSAN TOO*)* Oh, come on.

SUSAN TOO: Where will he sleep? What does he eat?

SUSAN: *(To* SUSAN TOO*)* We'll work out something. *(To* JAKE TOO*)* We'll work out something. *(Taking flower vase)* I'll get some water. *(Goes off left)*

JAKE TOO: I called Ted two days ago. To check it out. I made a point of calling.

SUSAN TOO: *(Snipping stems of flowers)* You'll have to excuse Ted. He's been a little distracted lately. He's in love.

JAKE TOO: You mean with Nancy?

SUSAN TOO: *I'll* say with Nancy. You know Nancy?

JAKE TOO: She came up to Dartmouth every weekend this spring.

SUSAN TOO: Well, then you know. You know what love can do.

JAKE TOO: He's been kind of spacey, all right.

SUSAN TOO: There you are.

*(*SUSAN *returns with flower vase, takes flowers, crosses to put them on table behind loveseat)*

SUSAN: Maybe he told me and it slipped my mind. Who knows? I've been a little spacey myself lately.

SUSAN TOO: For various reasons.

SUSAN: Which have nothing to do with love.

SUSAN TOO: I seem to be of two minds about almost everything.

JAKE TOO: I know the feeling.

SUSAN TOO: You too?

JAKE TOO: Especially when it comes to girls.

SUSAN TOO: With me, it's because I'm trying desperately to do something different in my work.

SUSAN: But that's *my* problem. *Your* problem is, where are you going to sleep.

SUSAN TOO: There's only one bed in Ted's room, so I'll have to put you in the girls' room.

SUSAN: They've left the nest, so it's all yours.

SUSAN TOO: If you can clear a path through the debris.

SUSAN: Maybe you should stay up here.

JAKE TOO: Here?

SUSAN TOO: *(Aside to* SUSAN*)* Here?

SUSAN: Why not? *(To* JAKE TOO*)* That daybed is perfectly comfortable and you'll have your own bathroom. With a working shower.

SUSAN TOO: *(Aside to* SUSAN*)* But I might want to work here.

JAKE TOO: But, hey, this is your studio.

SUSAN: That's all right. You'll be out painting houses during the day and I don't work here at night.

SUSAN TOO: *(To* JAKE TOO*)* I'll get you a blanket.

SUSAN: There you go.

(SUSAN TOO *goes off left)*

JAKE TOO: *(Looking around)* It's great up here, I'll say that . . . Light . . . Plenty of space . . .

SUSAN: It used to be the maid's room. Two maids' rooms, actually. Ted's father had it all done over to keep me happy while he commuted to Philadelphia.

JAKE TOO: So you could work, huh?

SUSAN: Oh yes. And it turned out I *had* to when he joined a commune in Vermont.

JAKE TOO: Ted says you've made it all on your own.

SUSAN: Well, here I was, stranded in the suburbs, with three small children . . .

JAKE TOO: *(Indicating her bulletin board)* And a talent to draw, huh?

SUSAN: A small talent.

JAKE TOO: Ted says you were the one who designed that little face that says, "Have a good day."

SUSAN: Ted exaggerates.

JAKE TOO: He says you have a major contract with Hallmark greeting cards.

SUSAN: I have a minor understanding with Hallmark greeting cards.

JAKE TOO: He says you're a major artist.

SUSAN: That's Ted.

(SUSAN TOO *returns with a blanket)*

SUSAN TOO: Ted has been my personal cheering section during some pretty tough times.

(She begins to make up the bed)

JAKE TOO: Well, that's what he says, anyway.

SUSAN TOO: Well, I'm not an artist.

SUSAN: Though I wish I were.

SUSAN TOO: I'm an illustrator. I copy other people's ideas. Repeat them. Pretty them up.

SUSAN: An artist looks at the world directly and tells us the truth.

SUSAN TOO: I don't do that. I look away.

SUSAN: I lie.

JAKE TOO: Oh come on.

SUSAN: *(Flipping through a stack of greeting cards)* I *do*. Look, come here. Fat little Santa Clauses. Coy little Easter bunnies. Hearts and flowers. That's me. Hearts and flowers for cocktail napkins and thank-you notes.

JAKE TOO: *(Picking up a card)* This one's cool.

SUSAN: No, it's no good. You see, no shadows, no darkness. It's all bright and light and easy . . .

SUSAN TOO: *(To* SUSAN, *coming downstage from the bed)* Where did I put that pillow?

SUSAN: I'll get it.

(She goes off up right)

SUSAN TOO: A friend once told me, a professor friend . . . how did he put it? I've devoted my career to cheering myself up. Well, in the process, I've tried to cheer up the American middle class. And pay the bills. And put three kids through college.

JAKE TOO: Way to go.

SUSAN TOO: Oh yes. I'm very proud of Sweet Sue. She's worked very
hard. I don't know where I'd be without her.

(SUSAN *returns with a pillow, putting it in a pillowcase*)

SUSAN: But this summer I intend to give her a break.

JAKE TOO: A break?

SUSAN: Yep. I intend to send her off on a good, long vacation.

SUSAN TOO: If I can.

SUSAN: Yep. Because this summer, while she's gone, I hope and pray I
can do one thing . . .

SUSAN TOO: One small thing . . . A drawing, a sketch even . . .

SUSAN: A flower . . . a tree . . .

SUSAN TOO: Yes, a tree . . . I'd love to draw a tree, which is totally,
totally . . .

SUSAN: True.

SUSAN TOO: If I can do that . . .

JAKE TOO: How will you know when you've done it? Will it be printed
in *The New York Times* or something?

SUSAN TOO: Oh sure!

SUSAN: You bet!

SUSAN TOO: No, I'll be able to tell, all by myself.

SUSAN: I'll just have a gut feeling. But I'll know. If it happens, I'll
know I'm good.

(*She returns to the drawing table*)

JAKE TOO: I've got a project for this summer, too.

SUSAN TOO: Yes, and I think you boys are wonderful, painting houses, earning money for college . . .

JAKE TOO: No, no, no, I didn't come here just to earn money, Mrs. Weatherill.

SUSAN TOO: What, then?

JAKE TOO: I came here because—*(He stops)* Forget it. I'll tell you when I know you better.

(Meanwhile SUSAN *has picked up the telephone on the drawing table and started dialing)*

SUSAN TOO: Well, then it's a crucial summer for both of us, isn't it? All the more reason to make yourself at home. Here. *(She gives him a towel)* Take a shower. Take *two* showers, like everyone else your age, and I'll see if I can locate Ted.

*(*SUSAN TOO *goes out up right.* JAKE TOO *goes out, tossing the towel to* JAKE, *who comes on from up right. He uses the towel to dry his hair. Meanwhile,* SUSAN *is putting down the telephone)*

SUSAN: *(Slamming down the telephone)* Well, he won't answer.

JAKE: Ted?

SUSAN: He won't answer the *phone.* Here his roommate suddenly arrives from out of town and he's totally incommunicado.

JAKE: That's O.K.

SUSAN: You see, he's over at Nancy's and both her parents work in the city. So Ted and Nancy spend the entire day . . . Well, I suppose you know this, you're his roommate . . . But they spend the entire day in bed together. *(Dials again)* Well, I'll just keep at it.

JAKE: Like Ted, huh?

SUSAN: What? Oh. Yes. *(Weak laugh, then listens on telephone) Now* they've put on that stupid answering machine: *(She mimics the machine)* "We are unable to come to the phone right now . . ." *I'll* say they're unable. *(Into the phone)* Ted, sweetheart, please call your mother. *(She hangs up irritatedly)*

JAKE: It's O.K., Mrs. Weatherill.

SUSAN: Honestly, those two.

JAKE: They get along better than any couple I know.

SUSAN: Too well, in my humble opinion.

JAKE: I envy them.

SUSAN: You do?

JAKE: I really do. To get along that well with another person . . . To connect that way all the time . . .

SUSAN: Oh, they connect, all right . . .

JAKE: A lot of people don't, though. A lot of people never do. Ever. In their entire lives.

SUSAN: A lot of people don't need to. Some people create a working partnership just with themselves.

JAKE: Yeah, I know. I read this book called *How to Be Your Own Best Friend.* That's O.K., I can live with that. But Ted and Nancy have it ten times better. I'd give my left . . . arm for a relationship like that. *(He crosses to the loveseat to put on his shoes)*

SUSAN: I suppose when she came up to Dartmouth, they kicked you out of your room.

JAKE: Ah, well, you know . . .

SUSAN: I mean, there you are paying perfectly good tuition, and not being able to sleep in your own bed.

JAKE: We worked it out. Really.

(He changes into a clean shirt at the bed)

SUSAN: Yes, well, I think there should be some restraints on these things. I'm all for sex, I think sex is a wonderful thing, but I don't think it has to consume . . . *(She notices his bare back, avoids looking, and continues)* . . . our every waking moment. We have rules in this house, Jake. I'll tell you that right now. We have very specific rules. I told the girls, I tell Ted *constantly:* This is not a hotel. He keeps wanting to have Nancy spend the night and the answer is no. What we do outside, out there in the wayward world, is our own business. But this house is sacrosanct, as far as I'm concerned. I like to think I've kept it an oasis of decency in a world gone absolutely haywire on the subject of sex. *(The telephone rings. She answers it immediately)* Hello, darling. Am I interrupting something? Well, guess who's here? Your best friend from Dartmouth . . . Yes, right here, and we've been having a lovely chat . . . So do you think you could possibly drag yourself over to join us? . . . Good. I'm so glad. Thank you, sweetheart. *(She hangs up, turns to JAKE)* He'll be right over.

JAKE: Oh yeah?

SUSAN: With Nancy.

JAKE: Great.

SUSAN: And I imagine they're very hungry.

(She goes quickly off up right, JAKE starts out down right as SUSAN TOO comes on in an apron, carrying a tray of ingredients for preparing dinner)

SUSAN TOO: Did you have a good day at work today?

JAKE: Same as usual.

SUSAN TOO: What color paint did you use?

JAKE: White. What else?

SUSAN TOO: Just wondered. Silly question. *(She gets a bowl from a nearby shelf.* HE *starts out again)* Where're you going?

JAKE: Out.

SUSAN TOO: Out?

JAKE: I thought I'd go to a movie.

SUSAN TOO: How will you get there? Didn't Ted take his car?

JAKE: I'll walk.

SUSAN TOO: Walk? In this town? You'll be violating the leash law.

JAKE: I'll take my chances.

SUSAN TOO: I suppose you could have my car.

JAKE: Nah . . .

SUSAN TOO: What'll you do about food?

JAKE: There's a pizza joint downtown.

SUSAN TOO: Don't you want to have a bite with me?

JAKE: Again?

SUSAN TOO: Why not?

JAKE: My mother said I should stay out of your hair.

SUSAN TOO: Don't be silly. Who likes to eat alone?

JAKE: *(Coming to the table)* I don't. That's for sure.

SUSAN TOO: Well, then . . . *(She begins to grate cheese. He sets the plates)* You'll have to put up with zucchini again tonight. Everyone grows it around here. And nobody likes it.

JAKE: I like it.

SUSAN TOO: Good.

JAKE: I like the way you cook it, anyhow.

(He takes a bite)

SUSAN TOO: Ted hates it.

JAKE: That's his problem.

SUSAN TOO: Not that it makes much difference. Seeing as how he eats over at Nancy's every night.

JAKE: Not every night.

SUSAN TOO: This is the second night in a row. He drops you off after work, then makes a beeline over to Nancy's.

JAKE: That's O.K.

SUSAN TOO: Still, you'd think he could at least wait to see Nancy until after dessert.

JAKE: Maybe Nancy *is* the dessert. *(Both laugh)* Actually, Ted and I made a deal this summer not to be a drag on each other.

SUSAN TOO: So you end up wandering off to the movies alone.

JAKE: I end up lucking out.

(A moment: she looks at him)

SUSAN TOO: Get yourself a beer, by the way.

JAKE: O.K. *(He goes upstage to get it from a shelf up right)* And the usual white wine for you?

SUSAN TOO: On the rocks this time, please. I got a slight buzz on last night.

JAKE: Come off it.

SUSAN: No, I did. You might not have noticed but I had three glasses. I probably bored you silly. Nattering on, like an old crone.

JAKE: *(Bringing the beer and wine)* I had a ball. Really. I did.

(They toast, glass to can)

SUSAN TOO: I suppose we'll have to do something about finding you a girl.

JAKE: I'll buy that.

SUSAN TOO: There's this sweet girl Jennifer Blum who's supposed to be around this summer.

JAKE: I met her.

SUSAN TOO: You met Jennifer?

JAKE: Does she teach swimming at the high school pool?

SUSAN TOO: I think she might.

JAKE: Goes to Hamilton? Kind of fat?

SUSAN TOO: Chubby?

JAKE: Chunky? Ted calls her Thunder Thighs?

SUSAN TOO: That's cruel. *(Pause)* But that's the one.

JAKE: I met her.

SUSAN TOO: And?

JAKE: No go.

SUSAN TOO: Didn't take?

JAKE: Mrs. Weatherill, I've got my problems with women.

SUSAN TOO: Oh well. Jennifer Blum is not God's only answer to mankind.

JAKE: No, but still . . . I've got my problems. I have great trouble establishing a meaningful relationship with them. I mean, I try to talk to them, I try to initiate a conversation, but to be honest with you, I give off these signals that I'm only interested in their bodies.

SUSAN TOO: Oh now.

JAKE: No, it's true. It's an old story with me, actually. My parents are serious Presbyterians, and ever since Sunday school, I've been trying to make up for lost time. Women pick up on it, Mrs. Weatherill. They all think I just want to jump their bones.

SUSAN TOO: Really?

JAKE: Sure. And the terrible thing about it is . . . it's true! But I'm fighting it, I swear. I'm really working on it. In fact, remember I told you I had a summer project? That's it. That's my project. That's why I'm here. To make myself establish a meaningful relationship with a woman. To see if I can learn to maintain eye contact with one for at least five minutes without glancing at her, well, breasts.

(SUSAN TOO *discreetly covers her chest*)

JAKE: *(Getting up, throwing down his napkin)* See? Now I've even made *you* nervous.

SUSAN TOO: No, no.

JAKE: Sure I have. Oh God. You know, I was planning to go to medical school up at Dartmouth. My dad's a pharmacist and he always wanted me to go one better and be a doctor. I was doing fine, too. I was passing organic chemistry and everything. But I gave it up, Mrs. Weatherill.

SUSAN TOO: Why?

JAKE: Because I can't get my head together about *women!* They could come in with an earache and I'd end up giving them a complete physical.

SUSAN TOO: I doubt that.

JAKE: Yeah, I'm exaggerating. My dad says I've just got normal human instincts. But wouldn't it be fantastic if you could take these instincts and commit them to one person all the time, all your life! I mean, my dad did that. I'd like to do it, too.

(He sits down at the table again)

SUSAN TOO: You'll find someone.

JAKE: You sound like my mom.

SUSAN TOO: Well, you will and she'll be very lucky.

JAKE: Thanks. *(They eat)* I'll bet there are a lot of guys hanging around you.

SUSAN TOO: Not many.

JAKE: Come on. I'm always hearing the phone ring . . .

SUSAN TOO: Mostly business.

JAKE: It rang tonight.

SUSAN TOO: You heard that?

JAKE: You were on for a long time.

SUSAN TOO: Bud Wainwright.

JAKE: Is he a big deal?

SUSAN TOO: Not so much any more.

JAKE: But you like him.

SUSAN TOO: In occasional doses.

JAKE: And he likes you, obviously.

SUSAN TOO: He likes baseball.

JAKE: So do I.

SUSAN TOO: Not like Bud. He *lives* the game. He has season tickets to Yankee Stadium and he's always dragging me along.

JAKE: Hey, wait a minute.

SUSAN TOO: What?

JAKE: He wanted to take you to the Yankee–Red Sox game tonight? And you turned him *down?*

SUSAN TOO: Yes.

JAKE: Jesus, Mrs. Weatherill! *Why?*

SUSAN TOO: I didn't want to go.

JAKE: Because of me?

SUSAN TOO: No.

JAKE: To keep me company?

SUSAN TOO: No!

JAKE: I'd feel terrible if you turned down a good seat at a major game because of me!

SUSAN TOO: Well, I didn't, Jake. I just wanted to stay home. Unlike you, I'm not quite so dependent on the opposite sex. *(Pause)* Oh, I was once, I suppose. Too dependent. The result was, I was married much too young and before I knew it, I had three small children.

JAKE: And then you found out what was causing it, right?

SUSAN TOO: *(Laughing)* I suppose you could say that . . . *(More seriously)* Well, I'm not young now. And I like very much being my own boss. Now. How about some ice cream? We have . . . Heavenly Hash or Cookie Crunch. Which?

JAKE: Both, please.

(JAKE TOO *enters with* Playboy *magazine, gets into the daybed.* SUSAN TOO *brings* JAKE *his ice cream)*

SUSAN TOO: Next time I'll ask Bud Wainwright to take you to the game instead.

JAKE: I dunno. Can't get ice cream like this at a ballpark.

(JAKE *eats as* SUSAN TOO *cleans up.* JAKE TOO *rolls over and falls asleep)*

JAKE: Actually, Mrs. Weatherill, I gotta tell you this: The reason I didn't eat over at Nancy's was I was hoping I could eat here again with you.

SUSAN TOO: I see.

JAKE: Sure. The movies were just a fall-back position. I didn't even know what was playing.

SUSAN TOO: Well, I'm glad you stayed.

JAKE: I mean, I'm torn. I'm into movies, I'm a movie freak sometimes, but I also like hanging out with you.

SUSAN TOO: Thank you, Jake.

JAKE: Want to go to the movies with me?

SUSAN TOO: Me? Tonight?

JAKE: So I can earn my keep around here?

SUSAN TOO: I don't like the movies much these days, Jake.

(SUSAN *enters eagerly*)

SUSAN: Unless it's something good.

SUSAN TOO: Which it never is.

JAKE: Where's the paper? Let's see what's playing. *(He gets a newspaper from a shelf, thumbs through it)* We'll find something, Mrs. Weatherill.

SUSAN: Well, if we're going out on a date, we'll make it Dutch treat. And you can at least call me Susan.

JAKE: Better not.

SUSAN: What's the matter?

JAKE: Ted doesn't want me to.

SUSAN: Ted?

JAKE: I asked him if I could call you by your first name and he said no.

SUSAN: Why not?

JAKE: He said he preferred the formalities.

SUSAN TOO: *(Who is finishing cleaning up)* Maybe it's just as well.

SUSAN: *(To* SUSAN TOO*)* Why?

JAKE: *(Reading newspaper)* This one's supposed to be a great. It's about a teen-age vampire ravaging a retirement home. All *right!*

SUSAN TOO: Think I'll skip that one, thanks.

JAKE: Just kidding. There's a French one down in the Village.

SUSAN: That's supposed to be marvelous!

JAKE: I'll get my jacket.

(He goes out right)

SUSAN TOO: I can't go.

SUSAN: *(Undoing* SUSAN TOO*'s apron)* Of course you can.

SUSAN TOO: What? Isn't that the one about this older woman who falls in love with an Algerian beach boy?

SUSAN: *(Fixing* SUSAN TOO*'s hair, as if they were standing together, facing a mirror)* You got it.

SUSAN TOO: You mean I should just show *up?* At the Fine Arts? With my son's *room*mate? Standing in line for tickets? Meeting the Wilsons and the Perlmutters head *on?*

SUSAN: Why not?

SUSAN TOO: What happens when we get inside? Do I behave like his *date?* Do I order one of those huge Cokes and suck noisily on a straw? . . . *(*SUSAN *takes off her own scarf, gags* SUSAN TOO *with it, and then adjusts it around her neck)* . . . Do we put our feet upon the seats in front of us and talk all during the show?

SUSAN: *(Standing back, looking at her)* There. You look gorgeous.

SUSAN TOO: What do I say to Bud Wainwright if he gets wind of this? Which he will. Knowing Bud.

SUSAN: I don't know. Tell him you're checking out the Little League.

SUSAN TOO: Oh, I can't! I just can't!

(JAKE *comes back on in a jacket*)

JAKE: All set?

SUSAN: Absolutely. Can't wait. *(Hands him the keys)* You do the driving, sir. *(Their hands touch. There is a brief moment of slow motion. Then* SUSAN *gives* SUSAN TOO *a gentle push.* SUSAN TOO *exits hesitantly, looking back, followed by* JAKE. SUSAN *remains onstage, watching them go. For a moment, she looks longingly at* JAKE TOO, *who lies on the cot, asleep. Then she crosses to a shelf and brings her drawing equipment back onto the table)* It's raining, it's pouring, the old man is snoring.

JAKE TOO: *(Rolling over, half awake)* Wumph.

SUSAN: It's raining. You can't paint houses today.

JAKE TOO: *(Sitting up suddenly)* What time is it?

SUSAN: Late. Almost eleven. Ted's off buying turpentine or something.

JAKE TOO: How come he didn't wake me up?

SUSAN: I told him to let you sleep.

JAKE TOO: Guess you want to work here, huh?

SUSAN: Guess I have to.

JAKE TOO: I'll get dressed in the john then.

(He exits right, covering himself with the bedclothes. SUSAN *begins to work at the drawing table)*

SUSAN: *(Calling off)* Did you hear the little argument downstairs this morning?

JAKE TOO: *(Offstage)* What?

SUSAN: There was a small argument at the breakfast table.

JAKE TOO: *(Offstage)* What about?

SUSAN: I'm not sure. Ted was in a terrible mood. That's why I wouldn't let him wake you.

JAKE TOO: *(Offstage)* Maybe he had a fight with Nancy.

SUSAN: No, I don't think it was Nancy. *(She organizes her work as she talks)* I think it was you. I think he's jealous of you. I really do. He's been cock of the walk around here for the past few years and now suddenly there's this other man sitting at the table, taking his mother to the movies, all that. I suppose Freud has something to tell us here. But it made for quite a little scene at the breakfast table, I can tell you that. Not that your name ever came up. Oh no. Never. It was all about why were the cornflakes soggy. And why couldn't we get a VCR. And why couldn't Nancy spend the night in his room. But you were the hidden agenda. I'm sure of that. *(Pause)* Did you hear me?

(JAKE TOO *comes partly out from offstage, hair wet, a towel around his waist)*

JAKE TOO: You were saying something, Mrs. Weatherill?

SUSAN: Just chattering on.

JAKE TOO: I was in the shower.

SUSAN: Probably just as well. *(He goes back off)* Though I do want to bring up a little plan I've been hatching. Can you hear me now?

JAKE TOO: *(Offstage)* I can hear.

SUSAN: I was going to ask you if you wanted to earn a little extra money in your spare time.

JAKE TOO: *(Offstage)* There's not much spare time, actually.

SUSAN: Oh, sure there is. Late afternoons . . . Sundays . . . Rainy days like today. (JAKE TOO *comes out still in his towel, partially covered with shaving cream, holding a razor)* I thought you might want to earn a little extra cash, that's all.

JAKE TOO: Doing what?

SUSAN: Modeling. *(Pause)* For me. *(Pause)* For my work. *(Pause)* When I'm not drawing trees.

JAKE TOO: You mean . . . posing?

SUSAN: Exactly.

JAKE TOO: No thanks, Mrs. Weatherill.

SUSAN: No?

JAKE TOO: No.

(He starts off)

SUSAN: Probably just as well. The way Ted's behaving these days, he'd go through the roof.

JAKE TOO: I'd never do it anyway, so there's no problem.

SUSAN: Fair enough. *(He is almost off)* May I ask why not?

JAKE TOO: I'd be embarrassed, Mrs. Weatherill.

SUSAN: Why?

JAKE TOO: You mean naked, don't you?

SUSAN: Not necessarily.

JAKE TOO: I'd still be embarrassed.

SUSAN: That's silly.

JAKE TOO: Yeah, well, I would be.

(He goes off)

SUSAN: *(Leaving her work, crossing right toward "the bathroom")* Now *that* is what I call the Sweet Sue Syndrome. I'm serious. I'm beginning to think we're all a little too prudish . . . *(She inadvertently looks off right at* JAKE TOO *in the bathroom, then quickly moves downstage)* . . . around here. Me included. I told Ted, I told him just this morning, that I intend to stop making cracks about him and Nancy. That's his business and it's fine. I also insist on a little reciprocity. If everyone else is going through some rite of passage this summer, why can't I? *(She furtively takes a pill, with water)* I mean, this is an important summer for me too, you know. My last child is leaving fast. My work is lately a little the worse for wear. My sense of personal well-being . . . *(She puts the pills away)* . . . leaves something to be desired. And what do I want to do about it? I want to stretch, that's what. I want to draw the human form occasionally. I want to develop my craft somewhat beyond the level of Porky Pig! And why the hell *can't* I? I don't see why Ted has to be the secret police around here?

(JAKE TOO comes out, buttoning his shirt)

JAKE TOO: Since Ted is out every night, maybe I'd better get into some good summer reading.

SUSAN: Maybe you'd better.

JAKE TOO: *(Tossing* Playboy *into the wastebasket after kissing it goodbye)* Get rid of this *Playboy*.

SUSAN: Good for you.

JAKE TOO: What's your favorite book? I'll read that.

SUSAN: My favorite? Oh, it's much too long for you.

JAKE TOO: Tell me what it is and I'll read it.

SUSAN: Tolstoy's *Anna Karenina*. Try that on for size.

JAKE TOO: I read it already.

SUSAN: You did not.

JAKE TOO: I did so. Comp Lit. Sophomore year.

SUSAN: And did you like it?

JAKE TOO: I loved it.

SUSAN: You did not.

JAKE TOO: It's one of my favorite books, I swear.

SUSAN: *(Looking at him)* I'm amazed.

JAKE TOO: We should talk about it sometime.

SUSAN: I'd love to do that. Anytime.

JAKE: Actually, I'm better after I've eaten.

SUSAN: Go, go, go, go. (JAKE TOO *exits up right.* SUSAN *calls after him)* I'm absolutely amazed! Ted couldn't get past the second chapter!

(JAKE *enters from right with bedclothes. They make the bed together)*

JAKE: Ted and I had a big fight two days ago.

SUSAN: A fight?

JAKE: A big one. We were painting the Kaplans' screen porch and he threw a whole can of primer at me.

SUSAN: Good Lord. What was the issue?

JAKE: He thinks I suck up to you.

SUSAN: He thinks you what?

JAKE: Suck up. It means—

SUSAN: I know what it means.

JAKE: He's still mad about that extra brownie you gave me.

SUSAN: But you're the guest!

JAKE: He's still mad.

SUSAN: Good lord. I'll buy a whole stack of brownies this afternoon.

JAKE: Yeah, well, I doubt if that will do it, Mrs. Weatherill.

(He sits on the cot and puts on his shoes. JAKE TOO comes on from up right, carrying a carton of orange juice. The two JAKES surround her)

JAKE TOO: Maybe I do suck up to you.

SUSAN: That's ridiculous.

JAKE TOO: No kidding. Maybe I do. Do you think I hang around you too much?

SUSAN: No. Not at all. No.

JAKE TOO: Because I have such a great time whenever I'm with you. I think you're the greatest . . .

JAKE: I mean, of all my friends' mothers . . .

JAKE TOO: I think you're the best.

SUSAN: Thank you, Jake.

JAKE TOO: And I'll tell you something else . . .

JAKE: Maybe I better not . . .

JAKE TOO: No, I want to tell you. You were a big factor in my decision to come here this summer.

JAKE: Of course I wanted to earn money, meet a girl . . .

JAKE TOO: But I also wanted to see you again, after that dinner we had up at Dartmouth.

JAKE: It was a great dinner . . . sirloin steak . . . strawberry short-cake . . .

JAKE TOO: But we had such a good conversation, remember?

JAKE: Of course maybe I drank too much beer . . .

(SUSAN *waves him down*)

JAKE TOO: But I remember thinking, hell, here's quite a lady . . .

JAKE: I mean for someone's mom . . .

SUSAN: *(Wheeling on JAKE impatiently)* Ah, leave it alone, will you? *(To JAKE TOO sweetly)* Go on.

JAKE TOO: Oh, I don't know. All I know is if it hadn't been for you I'd have ended up working in my dad's drugstore this summer. I'd be handing out poison ivy lotion and suppositories. And now look at me: having an intense conversation with a terrific woman even before breakfast. I feel lucky as hell, Mrs. Weatherill.

SUSAN: Why, thank you, Jake.

(She goes to her drawing table)

JAKE: *(Grabbing* JAKE TOO*'s arm, taking him aside)* Hey, man, cool it! What're you doing? Making the moves on Ted's mom?

JAKE TOO: Just talking, that's all. Just saying things.

JAKE: Yeah, well, you make it sound like you want to get it on with her.

JAKE TOO: Oh Jesus. Did it come out that way?

JAKE: It sure did, man. I thought that's what we're trying to get away from this summer!

(He cuffs him and goes out indignantly, as SUSAN TOO *comes on in a bathrobe, carrying* Anna Karenina. *She settles on the loveseat down right and begins to read)*

SUSAN: *(Who has been clearing off the drawing table; to* JAKE TOO*)* I keep thinking about that evening.

JAKE TOO: At the Surf and Turf?

SUSAN: Do you remember what we talked about?

JAKE TOO: Sure. Don't you?

SUSAN: Music.

JAKE TOO: You told me all about opera.

SUSAN: *(Getting an album from a shelf)* And you told me all about the Talking Heads. I bought their album when I got back. I studied it religiously.

JAKE TOO: Did you like it?

SUSAN: A little. I'm beginning to like "Little Creatures."

Mary Tyler Moore and Lynn Redgrave

Photographs © 1987 Martha Swope

Lynn Redgrave and John K. Linton

Barry Tubb and Lynn Redgrave

Mary Tyler Moore and John K. Linton

JAKE TOO: Did you ever try dancing to it alone?

SUSAN: No. Should I?

JAKE TOO: Sure. If you want.

SUSAN: Maybe I will. Some night. Late. After a glass of wine. With the door locked.

JAKE TOO: Well, I went and took a music course second semester.

SUSAN: Did you learn about Puccini?

JAKE TOO: I learned about the tragic gap.

SUSAN: Well, we got along anyway. At the old Surf and Turf.

JAKE TOO: Still do, don't we? I'll bet we connect on a lot of things. Take that album cover. I'll bet you like that.

SUSAN: *(Looking at it)* Not much, actually.

JAKE TOO: What's wrong with it?

SUSAN: Let me show you something. *(Takes an old drawing from a low shelf and puts it on the table)* I did this in art school.

JAKE TOO: *(Looking at it)* Hey!

SUSAN: It's just an apple with a bite in it.

JAKE TOO: I like that bite!

SUSAN: It's *my* bite. Nobody else did a bite. But it helped me shade it . . . see? . . . darken it, thicken the whole thing.

JAKE TOO: Christ, you even drew teeth marks.

SUSAN: Sure. Otherwise it would just be another easy apple for the Hallmark printing presses.

JAKE TOO: I couldn't have this, could I?

SUSAN: Nope. Sorry. I need it. It's the last thing I did before I left school and got married. I look at it now and then to remind myself that I am capable of doing things which have . . . well, bite.

JAKE TOO: Maybe you'll do something else this summer.

SUSAN: Maybe. Maybe something different. Maybe something better.

(She puts the drawing away)

JAKE TOO: You'll do it.

SUSAN: You're very nice. Of all Ted's friends, I think you're one of the . . . Of course, I like all of Ted's friends . . . But I really think you're one of the nicest.

JAKE TOO: Even if I don't like opera?

SUSAN: Even if you won't model for me.

JAKE TOO: Know why I won't do that?

SUSAN: Why?

JAKE TOO: I'm scared it would turn me on.

SUSAN: *(Embarrassed)* Oh honestly.

JAKE TOO: It's true. Now you know.

SUSAN: Thank you, Jake.

JAKE TOO: Oh Christ, I've got to get myself a *girl!*

(JAKE TOO goes out quickly. SUSAN puts away her materials as the lights begin to shift to night. SUSAN TOO, on the loveseat, looks up from her book and calls out to her)

SUSAN TOO: Hey.

SUSAN: Who, me?

SUSAN TOO: What's going on here?

SUSAN: I don't know what you mean.

SUSAN TOO: Are you falling in love with him?

SUSAN: No! *(Pause)* I suppose you could say I'm a little . . . infatuated.

SUSAN TOO: I'll buy that.

SUSAN: Think it shows?

SUSAN TOO: I think it's beginning to.

SUSAN: Well, it's fresh. It's fun. It's romantic.

SUSAN TOO: It's dangerous.

SUSAN: Yes! I suppose you could say it's the courtship I never had.

SUSAN TOO: Courtships are supposed to *lead* somewhere.

SUSAN: I know . . . *(She sits beside* SUSAN TOO *on the loveseat)* Maybe I should get away for a few days.

SUSAN TOO: Good idea.

SUSAN: Visit Harvey Satterfield on the Vineyard.

SUSAN TOO: Now we're talking.

SUSAN: I'll call him in the morning. Tell him I want to play with someone my own age.

SUSAN TOO: That's the ticket.

SUSAN: Or am I running away from the situation?

SUSAN TOO: No.

SUSAN: I could be.

SUSAN TOO: Yes.

SUSAN: Well, what if I am? Is that the worst thing in the world? I'm sorry, but I'm not of the school which says as soon as you feel a spark of something, you immediately have to start fanning the flame! What's wrong with putting a damper on things?

SUSAN TOO: Nothing's wrong at all.

SUSAN: So I'll go to the Vineyard.

SUSAN TOO: Yes.

SUSAN: Throw a little saltwater on the situation.

SUSAN TOO: Yes!

SUSAN: And then come back and continue my work.

SUSAN TOO: Work.

SUSAN: My summer project. My tree. My series of trees.

SUSAN TOO: Right.

SUSAN: I'll do a whole damn forest if I have to.

SUSAN TOO: Good for you.

SUSAN: Three cheers for the Protestant ethic.

SUSAN TOO: Two cheers, anyway.

SUSAN: And I'll accomplish something good this summer, rather than fritter it all away on a hopeless flirtation with a kid half my age!

(SUSAN *puts a suitcase on the drawing table*)

SUSAN TOO: *(As a cheer)* Go, Susan!!

SUSAN: Right on!

SUSAN TOO: Where is he, by the way?

SUSAN: Out.

(JAKE *enters up left, tiptoeing, carrying his shoes as if he were coming down a hall, late at night*)

SUSAN TOO: At this hour?

SUSAN: It's late, isn't it?

SUSAN TOO: It's too late.

SUSAN: I couldn't agree more.

(*She goes off, as* JAKE *comes into the light*)

SUSAN TOO: That you, Jake?

JAKE: Just me, Mrs. Weatherill.

SUSAN TOO: Well, well. Home is the hunter.

JAKE: Huh?

SUSAN TOO: Not only are we painting houses this summer, but now we are painting the town.

JAKE: Checking the scene a little.

SUSAN TOO: I thought you were just going to play miniature golf.

JAKE: We stopped at a bar afterwards.

SUSAN TOO: So Ted told me.

JAKE: Hoisted a few.

SUSAN TOO: So Ted said. When he got home. Two hours ago.

JAKE: Yeah, well. Good night, Mrs. Weatherill. *(Starts off)*

SUSAN TOO: I hear you met a girl.

JAKE: Right.

SUSAN TOO: At this bar.

JAKE: Right.

SUSAN TOO: What fun.

JAKE: It was, actually.

SUSAN TOO: Did she give you a ride home?

JAKE: Yep.

SUSAN TOO: That was thoughtful. I mean, it's a long walk from the Red Devil Bar and Grill.

JAKE: Yeah, well. Good night, Mrs. Weatherill.

(He starts off again)

SUSAN TOO: I must say I am a tad concerned, Jake.

JAKE: About what?

SUSAN TOO: Going to bars.

JAKE: Oh come on.

SUSAN TOO: Drinking beer until all hours of the night. Riding around in cars with strangers.

JAKE: Nancy knew her.

SUSAN TOO: I wonder if Nancy knew her very well. I wonder if Nancy is particularly friendly with women who pick up strange men in bars.

JAKE: Mrs. Weatherill . . .

SUSAN TOO: I don't like it, Jake. Frankly, I was quite worried. You should realize that I am *in loco parentis* here.

JAKE: My parents would be asleep.

SUSAN TOO: Well, I'm not, Jake. I'm very much awake. I had another big argument with Ted about it. I told him he had no business leaving you there.

JAKE: I *asked* him to. I made him go without me.

SUSAN TOO: Why?

JAKE: So I could get to know this girl.

SUSAN TOO: And did you?

JAKE: A little.

SUSAN TOO: I still don't like it. You'll be exhausted tomorrow. You could fall off a ladder and kill yourself.

JAKE: I won't, Mrs. Weatherill. Good night.

(Once again, he starts off. SUSAN *enters in a bathrobe, carrying a similar volume of* Anna Karenina)

SUSAN: I thought you and I had a little date tonight.

JAKE: What?

SUSAN: I thought after you'd played miniature golf, you were going to rush back here for our long-awaited talk on *Anna Karenina.*

SUSAN TOO: *(From couch)* I thought that was the deal. *(She holds up the identical book)*

JAKE: Sorry. I forgot.

SUSAN: I've started it again. I'm almost halfway through.

JAKE: I'm sorry. We were having so much fun at the bar, I forgot. Can we talk about it tomorrow?

SUSAN: *(Overlapping)* Well, I guess if having fun in the bar takes precedence over your commitments . . . Well, that is typical of your generation, isn't it. Boy, talk about a tragic gap. It's a tragic gulf, as far as I'm concerned. It's a tragic chasm . . . *(Pronouncing the "ch")* or chasm . . . *(Pronouncing the "k")* or ravine, or whatever the hell it is.

(She goes out angrily. SUSAN TOO, *still on the couch, has taken a sip from a glass of white wine hidden on the table behind her)*

SUSAN TOO: I must say, Jake, that I hope I won't have to spend the rest of the summer waiting up.

JAKE: No way, Mrs. Weatherill.

SUSAN TOO: It seems to me I've spent most of my life waiting. Waiting for my parents to finish cocktails so we could eat. Waiting for my husband to come back from work. Waiting for my husband to come back. Waiting for my children after school. Waiting for a telephone call from Hallmark. Wait, everyone said. Be patient, be polite, be good and decent and true, and it will all fall into place.

JAKE: Mrs. Weatherill . . .

SUSAN TOO: I wonder how many women in the world have spent their lives waiting. *(She indicates her book)* Anna does. Even after she runs off with Vronsky, she spends most of her time waiting.

JAKE: That's true.

SUSAN TOO: Maybe she shouldn't have bothered.

JAKE: She had nothing to keep her at home.

SUSAN TOO: That's right. Nothing. Except her son.

JAKE: I dunno, Mrs. Weatherill. You can get carried away. To be honest with you, that's what happened to me tonight. I got carried away with this girl. And that's what happened to Anna Karenina. Sometimes you just gotta go with it. Or you're dead.

SUSAN TOO: Seems to me she's dead either way.

JAKE: Yeah, but at least she lived before she died.

SUSAN TOO: And you want to live too, don't you?

JAKE: Absolutely.

SUSAN TOO: So, you met a girl.

JAKE: Right.

SUSAN TOO: Is she attractive?

JAKE: Sort of.

SUSAN TOO: And you like her?

JAKE: Sort of.

SUSAN TOO: And she likes you?

JAKE: I guess.

SUSAN TOO: And she has a car.

JAKE: It's her dad's.

SUSAN TOO: *(Getting up)* Cars are wonderful things, aren't they?

JAKE: Sure.

SUSAN TOO: They have wheels, they have radios, they have backseats.

JAKE: Hey . . .

SUSAN TOO: No, no. I understand these things. I'm not *that* old. I didn't grow up B.C.—Before Cars.

JAKE: I know you didn't, Mrs. . . .

SUSAN TOO: Of course, then, we were all probably much too choosy about whose car we got into.

JAKE: Yeah, well . . .

SUSAN TOO: Sounds like you've found your meaningful relationship this summer.

JAKE: I don't know about that.

SUSAN TOO: Sounds to me like you have.

JAKE: I don't know.

SUSAN TOO: I suppose she'll be coming around the rest of the summer.

(SUSAN *enters from left with a stack of clothes which she slams onto the table)*

JAKE: Who knows?

SUSAN TOO: Coming around. Honking her horn. Eager to take you off for some hot and heavy times in the backseat of Daddy's car.

JAKE: Go easy, Mrs. Weatherill.

SUSAN TOO: Yes, well, I think you'd better get some sleep, Jake. You'll need it. *(She goes off, up left)*

JAKE: *(Calling after her)* Good night, Mrs. Weatherill.

(She doesn't answer. He goes off the opposite way. SUSAN *packs her suitcase briskly)*

SUSAN: *(Singing)* "Every star above
　　　　　Knows the one I love"

(JAKE TOO *appears from stage right. He is eating a messy-looking sandwich)*

JAKE TOO: Going places?

SUSAN: Yes. Exactly. I'm taking a long weekend. Didn't Ted tell you?

JAKE TOO: Guess he forgot. Want some peanut butter and banana?

(He offers her a bite of his sandwich)

SUSAN: No thanks . . . Anyway, you'll have to fare for yourselves this weekend. I'll be leaving in half an hour. And I doubt if I'll be back until late Sunday night.

JAKE TOO: Have a good time, Mrs. Weatherill.

(He starts out, right)

SUSAN: I will definitely try to . . . um, Jake . . . *(He stops)* I suppose all sorts of things will go on in this house while I'm gone.

JAKE TOO: Huh?

SUSAN: What was that movie you told me about?

JAKE TOO: *Risky Business?*

SUSAN: I suppose all sorts of risky business will go on in this house.

JAKE TOO: Oh no . . .

SUSAN: Oh yes. But I don't want to know about it.

JAKE TOO: O.K.

(He starts off again)

SUSAN: Jake— *(He stops)* I do have a couple of no-no's, however.

JAKE TOO: Shoot.

SUSAN: I don't want anyone sleeping in my bed, thank you very much.
I know it's the only double bed in the house and consequently very
tempting, but I don't want anyone in it, is that clear?

JAKE TOO: Yes, Mrs. Weatherill.

SUSAN: Nor do I want to come home and find the liquor supply totally
depleted.

JAKE TOO: O.K.

SUSAN: If you do have to drink liquor, I'd like to think you'll supply
your own.

JAKE TOO: O.K.

SUSAN: I'm willing to provide the beer for you and Ted when I'm
around, but I'm not going to actively contribute to the delinquency of
every strange type who shows up here the minute I turn my back.

JAKE TOO: Gotcha, Mrs. Weatherill.

SUSAN: As for drugs, I believe you've heard my opinion on *that* subject
many times.

JAKE TOO: Right. Gotcha. Noted, Mrs. Weatherill.

(JAKE TOO starts out as JAKE enters)

JAKE: Where're you going, by the way?

JAKE TOO: *(Returning)* Where *are* you going?

SUSAN: Just a weekend away.

JAKE TOO: Won't tell, huh?

SUSAN: A friend of mine just bought a house on the Vineyard.

JAKE TOO: The Vineyard?

JAKE: You mean, *Martha's* Vineyard?

SUSAN: The same.

(She continues to pack)

JAKE TOO: Whoa!

JAKE: Oh my God, you'll have a ball!

SUSAN: I hope so. We'll see.

JAKE TOO: Does she live near the beach?

SUSAN: Who?

JAKE TOO: Your friend.

SUSAN: It's a he, actually.

JAKE TOO: Oh yeah?

JAKE: It's a guy, huh?

SUSAN: It's an old friend.

(She packs)

JAKE: *(Teasingly)* Well well, Mrs. Weatherill. Going to get a little action.

SUSAN: Don't get fresh, Jake.

JAKE TOO: A little action.

SUSAN: I mean it, Jake! Don't get smart, please!

JAKE: Just kidding. Sorry.

SUSAN: *(Continuing to pack)* To answer your question, yes, he *does* live near the beach.

JAKE TOO: Oh boy.

SUSAN: It sounds like a lovely location. And I'm very much looking forward to a little sun and sea.

JAKE TOO: You'll get plenty of sun all right.

SUSAN: Well, at least the weather forecast is good.

(She is packing a bathing suit)

JAKE TOO: I mean, you won't need that.

(He indicates the bathing suit)

SUSAN: What are you talking about?

JAKE TOO: I hear nobody wears a bathing suit on Martha's Vineyard.

SUSAN: Don't be silly.

JAKE TOO: It's true.

JAKE: This guy from Massachusetts told me at school.

JAKE TOO: They all go in nude up there.

JAKE: Then they roll around in these mud baths.

JAKE TOO: It's a very sexy place, Mrs. W.

JAKE: James Taylor, Carly Simon, Jackie O. They all spend their time up there rolling in the mud, skinny-dipping, and getting it on.

SUSAN: I am visiting a professor of moral philosophy, Jake.

JAKE TOO: Bet you wish he taught biology.

SUSAN: I wish no such thing. He's an old friend. He got his divorce about the same time I got mine. We've seen each other off and on ever since.

JAKE TOO: You mean clothes off or clothes on?

SUSAN: Now *stop* that! That's very fresh, Jake. Really.

JAKE: Sorry.

(SUSAN *packs*)

SUSAN: He's a very nice man. Ask Ted. Ted knows him. Knows him and likes him. Everyone likes him, as a matter of fact. He's a very likable man.

JAKE: And he likes you, huh?

SUSAN: I think so, Jake. I hope so.

JAKE TOO: Likes you enough to invite you up for a sexy weekend on Martha's Vineyard.

SUSAN: All right, Jake. Have it your way. Yes.

(SUSAN TOO *comes on, carrying a beach bag and other items of clothing. She helps pack*)

SUSAN TOO: Actually, I invited myself.

JAKE: No kidding.

SUSAN TOO: He's an academic. He likes to read, look at birds, grow tomatoes. He doesn't always . . .

SUSAN: Make his move.

SUSAN TOO: Sometimes he has to be . . .

SUSAN: Prodded a little.

SUSAN TOO: Which, of course, is part of his charm.

SUSAN: Actually, it's a very different sort of thing, really.

SUSAN TOO: Very different.

SUSAN: I mean, we're older. We don't have to . . . We don't want to . . .

SUSAN TOO: We have other interests.

SUSAN: Exactly.

SUSAN TOO: Besides sex.

SUSAN: It's a generational thing, actually. Your generation is tyrannized by sex. You're bombarded with it day and night. Your music, your TV ads . . .

SUSAN TOO: You're obsessed by it. You think it's the be-all and the end-all. But it isn't.

SUSAN: I mean, I know sex . . .

SUSAN TOO: I'm no stranger to sex . . .

(She rubs her arms with suntan lotion)

SUSAN: Bud Wainwright and I had what you might call a . . .

SUSAN TOO: A sexual relationship.

SUSAN: After the baseball, we'd always go back to his condo and . . .

(Pause)

SUSAN TOO: The point is that there are other ways to connect to another human being . . .

SUSAN: Many other ways . . .

SUSAN TOO: You can read the same books, enjoy the same music . . .

SUSAN: Now this Vineyard gentleman and I have built up a very warm, very congenial relationship over the years . . .

SUSAN TOO: Very warm, very congenial . . .

SUSAN: He introduced me to opera, for example.

SUSAN TOO: Yes, we listen to opera together.

SUSAN: And there's very little sex involved at all.

(Pause. JAKE *and* JAKE TOO *look at each other)*

JAKE TOO: Better take your sketch pad. Maybe this professor will pose nude for you.

SUSAN TOO: I don't *have* to draw nudes, Jake.

SUSAN: I am drawing trees.

SUSAN TOO: Yes! You may not have noticed, but I am drawing some beautiful trees.

SUSAN: Which Harvey Satterfield would appreciate immediately.

JAKE: *(Starting out)* Yeah, well, I got a date tonight.

SUSAN: With your barroom companion?

JAKE: You got it.

SUSAN: Fine. Have a good time.

(JAKE *starts off, then comes back*)

JAKE: This Vineyard guy. Is he the one who said you were just cheering yourself up?

SUSAN: He's the one.

JAKE: Sounds like a jerk.

SUSAN TOO: Well, he's a very nice man.

JAKE: Well, he sounds like a very nice jerk.

(*He goes out right*)

SUSAN: (*Slyly, to* SUSAN TOO) I think he's actually jealous.

SUSAN TOO: Oh no.

SUSAN: Just a tad.

SUSAN TOO: No, no.

SUSAN: Oh yes yes yes. Now, where did I put that beach towel?

(*She goes out up right.* JAKE TOO *stays*)

JAKE TOO: Did you just call him up and say you were coming?

SUSAN TOO: Something like that.

JAKE TOO: Why?

SUSAN TOO: I needed a change of scene.

JAKE TOO: Why?

SUSAN TOO: I just did.

JAKE TOO: Because of me?

SUSAN TOO: No.

JAKE TOO: I'll bet because of me.

SUSAN TOO: No! Not at all. No.

JAKE TOO: Am I getting you down?

SUSAN TOO: Oh no . . .

JAKE TOO: Staying out half the night, pigging out in the kitchen, overloading the washing machine, forgetting to put gas in the car . . . No wonder you want to bug out.

SUSAN TOO: *(Crossing to loveseat for her book)* It's not that, Jake. I love having you here. Love it. It's just that I need to be with someone my own age. Just as you do, Jake. With that girl from the bar.

JAKE TOO: I don't like her that much.

SUSAN TOO: Oh now . . .

JAKE TOO: I don't. She's boring, Mrs. Weatherill.

SUSAN TOO: Well, she seems to be boring you pretty nearly every night.

JAKE TOO: That's just sex, Mrs. Weatherill.

SUSAN TOO: Oh come on.

JAKE TOO: I'm talking about, what I'm talking about . . . You've spoiled me, Mrs. Weatherill. She seems so dumb alongside you.

SUSAN TOO: Oh well . . .

JAKE TOO: I'm serious. I mean, she's waiting out in the car right now . . . *(He dashes to the window, waves frantically off right, and returns)* . . . and I don't even want to go. I'd rather stay here, talking to you.

SUSAN TOO: I think you should let me get going, Jake. *(She edges carefully around him)* I mean, I'm not Anna. You're not Count Vronsky. *(She goes to close the suitcase)* We've been living in rather close quarters around here, Jake. It's natural that people might become . . . well, infatuated. Do you know what that word means? Infatuated? I've recently had occasion to look it up. It means "made fatuous," Jake. "Made foolish." The best thing to do is just snap out of it. Get on with it. All that.

JAKE TOO: O.K.

SUSAN TOO: Talk to this girl about rock and roll or something.

JAKE TOO: Right.

SUSAN TOO: While I'm listening to opera with Harvey on the Vineyard.

JAKE TOO: Right.

(SUSAN returns with the beach towel, stands listening)

SUSAN TOO: Otherwise, we're just wandering around in the never-never land of infatuation.

JAKE TOO: Right. *(He starts out, stops, turns)* Still: If I were a professor with a house on Martha's Vineyard, I'd invite you up every weekend. I'd make it an open invitation. And I'd get into bed with you every chance I got.

(JAKE TOO goes off quickly. SUSAN looks at SUSAN TOO, then bursts into a sexy version of "Sweet Sue," using her towel as if she were a burlesque queen)

SUSAN TOO: *(Trying to stop her)* Hey. Quit that. Knock it off. Stop! He'll hear you! Susan Weatherill, don't be an absolute fool! (SUSAN

TOO *finally gets the towel from her, crosses to the table, with* SUSAN *imitating her all the way.* SUSAN TOO *packs the towel in the beach bag, starts off briskly, then stops, and looks at* SUSAN) I don't want to go now. (SUSAN *looks at* SUSAN TOO, *then takes a pill. They go off either way.* JAKE TOO *comes on with a beer and stands leaning against a shelf watching* SUSAN TOO *go off.* JAKE *comes on from the opposite side. He removes black paint from his hands)*

JAKE TOO: *(Looking off)* Did she have a good time?

JAKE: She said she did.

JAKE TOO: She came back early.

JAKE: Right.

JAKE TOO: *(Gives* JAKE *a slug of his beer)* I missed her.

JAKE: Oh God.

JAKE TOO: I missed her more than I thought I could miss a woman.

JAKE: Tell me about it.

JAKE TOO: Do you think she missed me?

JAKE: She said she did.

JAKE TOO: That could've been bullshit.

JAKE: Right . . .

(Pause)

JAKE TOO: What should I do about it?

JAKE: Do you want to . . . ?

JAKE TOO: No, I don't want to! I don't know what I want to do.

JAKE: Remember what Dad said: "Forget the women and earn the dough."

JAKE TOO: Right.

JAKE: And remember Mom's letter: "Change your underwear and trust in the Lord."

JAKE TOO: Oh Jesus. Maybe I'd just better shove off.

JAKE: Yeah, well, whatever you decide, make sure you check it out with Ted.

JAKE TOO: You check it out with Ted, smart-ass. Shit, lot of help *you* are.

(He goes off up right, as SUSAN *comes on briskly in an apron from down left with cooking ingredients)*

SUSAN: Hi.

JAKE: Hi.

SUSAN: *Black* paint today?

JAKE: We're finishing up the Kaplans' shutters.

SUSAN: Ah.

(She breaks the eggs into the bowl)

JAKE: *(Looking at her)* Making a cake?

SUSAN: From the ground up. If I can remember how to do it.

JAKE: You remind me of my mom.

SUSAN: *(Not pleased)* Really?

JAKE: She's always in the kitchen baking cakes for the church.

SUSAN: Well, of course this is for Ted.

JAKE: Ted?

SUSAN: It's his birthday. Didn't he tell you?

JAKE: No.

SUSAN: Well, it is. It's his twenty-first. Didn't he even tell you Nancy was coming to dinner?

JAKE: No.

SUSAN: Well, she is. And so is Harvey Satterfield.

JAKE: Harvey Satterfield?

SUSAN: My professor friend. He's coming in especially from the Vineyard.

JAKE: Ted didn't tell me any of that.

SUSAN: Well, it's all happening and we're having his favorite meal, including a homemade cake . . . *(Looking at an ingredient)* . . . if I can remember how to do it. And in a few minutes I'm going to ask you to drive down and pick up some of his favorite ice cream.

(JAKE *sits on the stool downstage to change out of his painting shoes*)

JAKE: I don't think he wants me here.

SUSAN: Ted?

JAKE: He would've told me about the party.

SUSAN: Ted is extremely distracted this summer.

JAKE: I think he'd be just as glad if I shoved off.

SUSAN: Well, you can't, anyway. You haven't finished the Kaplans' house and you've got that mammoth Victorian of the Millworths' still to go.

(She works on the cake)

JAKE: Ted's thinking of subcontracting that job.

SUSAN: *Sub*contracting? What does that mean, subcontracting?

JAKE: There's this guy Bobby Peretti who's also painting houses this summer. Ted's thinking of subcontracting the job to him.

SUSAN: And why would he want to do that?

JAKE: He wants to take Nancy camping in Vermont.

SUSAN: He wants to do what?

JAKE: Take Nancy camping. Maybe it's a birthday present. To himself.

SUSAN: And will he see his father?

JAKE: Didn't say.

SUSAN: Who lives in a *trailer?* Near *Rut*land? With God knows *what?*

JAKE: Didn't say, Mrs. Weatherill.

SUSAN: But what happens to you? Would you work for this Peretti person?

JAKE: He has his own crew.

SUSAN: But that leaves you high and dry!

JAKE: I could go home. Work in my dad's drugstore.

SUSAN: Why, that's outrageous!

JAKE: It's cool.

SUSAN: It is *not* "cool." Ted made a deal to do the Millworths'.

JAKE: It might be better this way, Mrs. Weatherill. Really. Ted and I aren't getting along these days. To be honest with you, we argue about stupid stuff all the time. So maybe it's better to split before we start working on a whole new house.

SUSAN: No! I do not agree with that. No! *(She angrily beats the cake batter, walking around the room)* We do not make contracts and then walk out on them. No. We do not invite our roommates to visit us for the summer and then suddenly send them packing! No. We do not make very specific arrangements to paint our friends' houses and then hand things over to a complete stranger! Oh no! I'm sorry. That's something we do not do.

JAKE: Bobby Peretti's very good. He plans to make painting his profession!

SUSAN: I don't care if he's Michelangelo! We stick to our obligations in this family! Honestly. That Ted. He's just like his father. Things get a little difficult, a little emotionally complicated, and he wants to walk away from the whole shebang! *(She returns to the table)*

JAKE: Look, maybe tonight I should just shove off and eat a pizza.

SUSAN: NO! We are going to have a pleasant meal tonight—*all* of us! *(Goes to shelf)* Now please. Here's ten dollars. Drive down and get some of that ice cream with the Oreos in it, and then come back and change your clothes. Please, Jake. This is very important to me.

JAKE: *(Taking the money)* O.K.

(He goes off right, as SUSAN puts the batter on the shelf. SUSAN TOO comes out center, now dressed for the party. She adjusts her dress as if in front of a full-length mirror)

SUSAN: You're not going to wear that, are you?

SUSAN TOO: Why not?

SUSAN: Don't you think it's a bit much?

SUSAN TOO: *(Looking in the mirror)* Much?

SUSAN: Much. Much. Do you know what the word means? I've recently had occasion to look it up.

(She exits left as JAKE TOO enters from behind and watches SUSAN TOO adjusting her dress in the mirror)

JAKE TOO: "Mirror, mirror on the wall . . ."

SUSAN TOO: *(Startled)* Oh, Jake . . .

JAKE TOO: *(Coming toward mirror)* Who is the fairest of them all? Maybe it's Mrs. Weather-all.

SUSAN TOO: Why, thank you, Jake.

JAKE TOO: Here's your change from the ice cream.

(He holds out his hands in fists. She slaps his left hand. He opens it. It is empty. He shows her his right containing the money)

SUSAN TOO: Oh, keep it. Go buy yourself a car.

JAKE TOO: Right.

(JAKE TOO *starts off right. Then stops)*

JAKE TOO: Could I ask you a serious question?

SUSAN TOO: All right.

JAKE TOO: Did you love your husband?

SUSAN TOO: Oh yes. For a while. Yes.

JAKE TOO: Did he love you?

SUSAN TOO: He said he did.

JAKE TOO: Why did he leave you, then?

SUSAN TOO: Oh, Jake, it's a long story.

JAKE TOO: I think I know why. He thought you were too good for him. I'll bet that was why he split.

SUSAN TOO: Oh God, I hope that isn't true.

JAKE TOO: Or maybe he just thought you were too good-looking.

SUSAN TOO: Thank you, Jake. Do you think I'm wearing too much makeup?

JAKE TOO: *(Looking at her in mirror)* I like you without any makeup at all.

SUSAN TOO: Well, thanks again.

JAKE TOO: Sure. I can appreciate a good antique . . . Just kidding.

SUSAN TOO: Get dressed, Jake. They'll be here.

(JAKE TOO *goes off right as* JAKE *comes on, now in a jacket*)

JAKE: This O.K.?

SUSAN TOO: Wonderful.

JAKE: Think I should put on a tie?

SUSAN TOO: You look fine.

(SUSAN TOO *begins to spread a tablecloth on the drawing table*)

JAKE: Can I help?

SUSAN TOO: You can get the dishes . . . I'm pulling out all the stops tonight. My grandmother's silver, the works . . . This is what is called "putting on the dog."

(JAKE *helps her set the table*)

JAKE: Woof, woof.

SUSAN TOO: Oh—and Jake . . .

JAKE: Hmmm?

SUSAN TOO: You and I should make a special effort tonight.

JAKE: To do what?

SUSAN TOO: Not to talk.

JAKE: Not to *talk?* At a *party?*

SUSAN TOO: To each *other*, Jake.

JAKE: Oh.

SUSAN TOO: I mean sometimes you and I get rolling.

JAKE: *Some*times? All the time.

SUSAN TOO: On *Anna Karenina*, for example.

JAKE: *Or* movies. *Or* politics. *Or* even baseball.

SUSAN TOO: You see? Ted says we monopolize the meal.

JAKE: Right.

SUSAN TOO: So we have to be careful, Jake. We have to concentrate on Ted.

JAKE: Right.

SUSAN TOO: Because this is his night, after all. We're all here to tell him that. We all love him and there's no need for anyone to go running off into the woods.

JAKE: Gotcha, Mrs. Weatherill.

SUSAN TOO: And no need for anyone to run home to Daddy's drugstore, either.

JAKE: Yeah, well . . .

SUSAN TOO: No, I'm serious. We're all in this thing together.

(SUSAN *enters from left with two bottles of wine, she is also dressed up*)

SUSAN: Which does not mean we have to baby him, either.

SUSAN TOO: Oh no. I don't mean that.

SUSAN: After all, he is twenty-one years old now. He is a grown-up. Like the rest of us.

SUSAN TOO: Just like you, Jake.

JAKE: Oh, I'm older, actually.

BOTH SUSANS: *(Hopefully)* Really?

JAKE: Yeah. Actually, I'm almost twenty-three.

SUSAN: Hmm . . . Well . . .

SUSAN TOO: I see.

SUSAN: Well, the point is, we are all mature human beings. And I think it's time to loosen the leash a little.

SUSAN TOO: Give people a little more leeway.

SUSAN: For example, tonight I plan to tell Ted that he can have Nancy sleep over occasionally.

SUSAN TOO: If he wants.

SUSAN: If she wants.

SUSAN TOO: Occasionally.

SUSAN: As long as they're discreet about it.

SUSAN TOO: If it's all right with her family, it's fine with me.

SUSAN: Even if it isn't all right, that's their problem.

SUSAN TOO: Do you agree, Jake?

SUSAN: I mean, I can't play policeman for the entire world.

SUSAN TOO: I mean, if people want to sleep together, why the hell not?

SUSAN: I might even get Ted a bigger bed.

SUSAN TOO: A bigger bed?

SUSAN: It might just ease the tension around here.

SUSAN TOO: For all of us.

SUSAN: People might stop being so prickly and argumentative.

SUSAN TOO: You might even model for me, Jake.

JAKE: I doubt it, Mrs. Weatherill.

SUSAN TOO: You might.

JAKE: I doubt it.

(The telephone rings)

SUSAN TOO: I'll get it.

(She goes upstage to answer it)

SUSAN: I'll bet poor old Harvey missed the ferry yet again.

SUSAN TOO: It's for you, Jake.

JAKE: Oh yeah?

SUSAN TOO: I suspect it's your little friend from the bar.

(She hands him the phone)

SUSAN: Tell her you're tied up—all night long.

(JAKE *talks with his back to the audience.* JAKE TOO *comes on, now similarly dressed up. He carries something behind his back)*

JAKE TOO: Mrs. Weatherill, I've got a present for you.

SUSAN: For me?

SUSAN TOO: This is Ted's birthday, not mine.

JAKE TOO: I don't care. I was going to give it to you when I left, but I decided to do it now. *(He hands it to* SUSAN) Maybe it's better than those wimpy flowers I brought when I arrived.

SUSAN: It's a record album!

SUSAN TOO: *(Reading the title) Old Favorites.*

JAKE TOO: Read the third selection.

SUSAN: *(Reading)* "Sweet Sue!"

SUSAN TOO: Where did you find it?

JAKE TOO: In New York. The weekend you went to Vineyard. See? I didn't have an orgy, after all.

SUSAN: *(Reading more titles)* Oh—and look! Cole Porter, Richard Rodgers, everything.

JAKE TOO: I bought it because it had "Sweet Sue."

SUSAN TOO: *(Taking it to the record player)* Let's play it.

SUSAN: Oh yes!

JAKE TOO: It's a tough song to find, I'll say that. I went to all those old record stores and I finally found it at a place called Bleecker Bob's.

(The music comes up: a lively rendition of "Sweet Sue." SUSAN begins to sway, then dance. SUSAN TOO follows suit)

JAKE TOO: *(After a moment)* Want to dance?

SUSAN TOO: Now?

JAKE TOO: Before Ted comes back.

SUSAN: All right.

(JAKE TOO and SUSAN start to dance)

JAKE TOO: I'm not too good at couple-dancing.

SUSAN: You're fine.

SUSAN TOO: *(Watching)* You're terrific.

JAKE TOO: *(Spinning her off)* I learned this from my mother.

SUSAN: *(Stopping for a moment)* Let's forget your mother, shall we? *(She dances closer to him)*

SUSAN TOO: *(Watching)* Oh, this brings back such memories. When I was your age, we all used to dance all the time. That's how we got to know a person. By dancing. You'd dance with a man and you could tell. That's how I met Ted's father. I was at a party and he cut in on me and before I knew it, he had danced me right off my feet . . .

(SUSAN TOO *and* JAKE TOO *dance well together. Then* JAKE *hangs up the phone and for a moment, watches them dance, then comes downstage)*

JAKE: *(Low, to* JAKE TOO*)* Ask her.

JAKE TOO: *(Low, over his shoulder)* Not yet.

JAKE: *(Coming down, grabbing his arm)* You gotta ask her!

JAKE TOO: *(Dancing* SUSAN *away)* I said not *yet.*

SUSAN: What's the matter?

JAKE TOO: Nothing.

(He spins her off. JAKE *cuts in: to be there when she spins back.*

JAKE: *(After dancing with her for a moment)* Mrs. Weatherill, could I please borrow your car?

SUSAN: *(Stopping dancing)* My car?

SUSAN TOO: For what?

JAKE: Tonight.

JAKE TOO: A little later.

JAKE: Right now.

JAKE TOO: Sorry.

(Pause)

SUSAN TOO: *(Crossing to record player)* I'd better turn this thing off.

(The music stops)

JAKE: *(Low, to* JAKE TOO*)* Tell her.

JAKE TOO: *You* tell her.

SUSAN: Hey. What's going on.

JAKE: Mrs. Weatherill, when I was down getting the ice cream, I met this girl.

SUSAN TOO: What girl?

JAKE TOO: She mixes the Oreos into the ice cream.

JAKE: I asked her out, Mrs. Weatherill.

SUSAN: *Tonight?*

JAKE TOO: So I wouldn't be a drag around here.

JAKE: And she just called and said yes.

JAKE TOO: She's waiting for me.

JAKE: So I need a car.

SUSAN TOO: But the party . . .

JAKE TOO: I'd be a fifth wheel here, really.

JAKE: Oh, hey, lookit, Mrs. Weatherill. I was planning to shove off tomorrow.

JAKE TOO: I planned to give you that record tomorrow and split.

SUSAN TOO: I see.

JAKE: But this girl . . .

JAKE TOO: Elaine . . .

JAKE: . . . She changes everything. I mean it was dynamite! We connected immediately!

JAKE TOO: We had a really good conversation even while she was getting the ice cream!

JAKE: And when she called just now, we were so eager to talk we could hardly get off the phone!

JAKE TOO: So I decided to give you that record tonight, Mrs. Weatherill.

JAKE: I want to stay here this summer.

JAKE TOO: I want to try to develop this relationship.

JAKE: And you know what, Mrs. Weatherill? There could be a whole different atmosphere around here now. This could be a whole new ball game.

JAKE TOO: If I can just have your car.

(SUSAN *looks at* SUSAN TOO, *then points to the keys on the table behind the loveseat*)

SUSAN: All right.

JAKE TOO: Oh thanks, Mrs. Weatherill.

(*He rushes out, tossing the keys in the air*)

JAKE: Thanks. Really.

(*He kisses* SUSAN *impulsively on the cheek, then goes out too.* SUSAN *stands looking after them, holding her cheek*)

(Pause)

SUSAN: It's hot in here.

SUSAN TOO: Something's burning.

SUSAN: Yes.

SUSAN TOO: Oh Lord, it's the cake!

SUSAN: No, it's not. I'm burning. It's me.

QUICK CURTAIN

Act Two

Act Two

ACT TWO

(The stage looks the same as it did at the beginning of Act One. Only this time it is JAKE TOO *who is posing in the nude on a stool, while* SUSAN TOO, *in jeans and a smock, draws him at the drawing table.* SUSAN *stands upstage, looking out the window)*

SUSAN TOO: *(As she sketches)* This might have been the way to end it, Jake.

JAKE TOO: I doubt it, Mrs. Weatherill.

SUSAN TOO: Oh come on. It might have solved everything.

JAKE TOO: What about Ted, Mrs. Weatherill?

SUSAN TOO: Ted? Who's Ted?

JAKE TOO: Six-foot-three? Likes brownies?

SUSAN TOO: Oh, that Ted.

JAKE TOO: That Ted.

SUSAN TOO: Ted understands I'm an artist. He used to pose for me all the time.

JAKE TOO: Yeah, but not like this!

SUSAN TOO: He'd understand I'm trying to grow in my work. It wouldn't bother Ted.

SUSAN: *(From window)* Dreaming again?

SUSAN TOO: Trying to.

SUSAN: Talk about dreams, the boys are playing Frisbee on the lawn. What a beautiful game!

SUSAN TOO: *(To* JAKE TOO*)* You see? You and Ted are getting along fine these days.

JAKE TOO: Since Elaine.

SUSAN TOO: Elaine?

JAKE TOO: My girl.

SUSAN TOO: Ah. Miss Heavenly Hash.

SUSAN: *(At window)* It's as if they were in perpetual slow motion.

SUSAN TOO: *(To* JAKE TOO*)* Does Ted like Elaine?

JAKE TOO: He likes it that I like her.

SUSAN: No rules, no lines, no one keeping score . . .

SUSAN TOO: *(To* JAKE TOO*)* Well, it's nice to know we've appeased Ted.

SUSAN: *(Coming downstage)* I think everyone in the world should play Frisbee. It's the solution to world peace. *(To* SUSAN TOO*)* Do the Russians play?

SUSAN TOO: I have no idea.

SUSAN: Well, they should. We should send great batches of Frisbees to the Russians and South Africa. I think the Ayatollah Khomeini should be forced to play Frisbee.

SUSAN TOO: Would you be quiet, please? I am trying to draw.

SUSAN: *(She returns to the window)* Now they've stopped, anyway. Oh, I hate to see it end. But they're probably hungry again.

(She goes off right. JAKE TOO *wraps his towel around himself)*

SUSAN TOO: Now what's the matter?

JAKE TOO: I keep worrying about Ted. *(He gets up)* Maybe I should put on a bathing suit or something.

SUSAN TOO: Don't be silly. Sit down. Please. (JAKE TOO *does, reluctantly, with the towel wrapped around him.* SUSAN TOO *tries to continue drawing)* Just forget about Ted. After all, Ted forgets about us. Or will, before too long. He'll graduate next year, he'll be gone, and I'll be lucky if I get a call from him once a month. Fine. That's life. Good-bye, Ted. He's free, I'm free, that's that. *(She draws frantically, then stops)* Ted, Ted, Ted. Why does Ted brood over my life, like some God? Are we doomed to be forever at the mercies of our own children? Will there never be a time when we're free? *(She gets up, crosses to the drawing table, erases what she has drawn)* One of the reasons I got married so young was to get out from under the disapproving frowns of my parents. Am I now to spend the rest of my days kow-towing to my kids? Oh sure, when they were growing up, I was responsible. I couldn't go tearing around. I couldn't afford to send them reeling onto the couches of the local psychiatrists. But now they're old, they're on their own, they're fine. I've got a daughter living with a twice-divorced Italian in California. I've got another involved in some bizarre ménage in New York. And now Ted's shacking up right here, right under my nose. I don't pry, I don't criticize. I don't burst through that constantly closed bedroom door and scatter moral disapproval all over the rug. He has his life, why can't I have mine? Why the hell can't I take pencil in hand and draw a few sketches of a naked man? Good Lord, am I doomed to be Sweet Sue until the day I *die? (She resumes her seat, tries to draw again)*

JAKE TOO: I don't know, Mrs. Weatherill.

SUSAN TOO: And why can't you ever call me Susan?

JAKE TOO: I'll try, Mrs. Weatherill. I mean, I'll try, Susan.

(SUSAN *re-enters quickly)*

SUSAN: Because I'll tell you frankly, Jake, I doubt I'll ever create a major work of art knowing I'll end up signing it "Mrs. Weatherill."

SUSAN TOO: We need a little music here.

SUSAN: Opera? Again?

SUSAN TOO: No, it doesn't work. Play "Sweet Sue."

SUSAN: No, I'm trying to get *away* from "Sweet Sue."

SUSAN TOO: *(To* JAKE TOO) Did I ever tell you how I got hooked on that song?

SUSAN: My father had the sheet music. He used to keep it on the piano.

SUSAN TOO: And whenever I'd get upset or angry . . .

SUSAN: Why he'd call me into the living room and sit me down at the piano bench beside him . . . (SUSAN TOO *sings quietly underneath)* You see, I used to be a terrible little girl . . .

JAKE TOO: Oh come on.

SUSAN: No, I was. I was a complete hellion. I used to wander around the house, causing trouble. But if my father were home, he'd sit me down beside him on the piano bench and play.

SUSAN TOO: *(Singing quietly)* "Every star above . . . Knows the one I love . . ."

SUSAN: "Sweet Sue . . . Just—" *(She stops, snaps out of it)* And that would calm me down, so I could do my homework.

SUSAN TOO: He's dead now. And now I'm a little too old to be crooned to.

(She hands the drawing to SUSAN, *who takes over)*

JAKE TOO: Well, I guess you don't get upset much any more, anyway.

SUSAN: Oh, I do.

SUSAN TOO: You don't know . . .

SUSAN: Don't be snowed by all this Sweet Sue stuff.

SUSAN TOO: Why do you think I take those pills?

SUSAN: Sue's sweetness is sometimes chemically induced.

SUSAN TOO: And carefully maintained with appropriate doses of white wine.

SUSAN: Underneath, there's a very different person.

SUSAN TOO: Or twenty different people, frantic to get out.

SUSAN: I think that's why I like opera so much. All those different voices singing at the same time.

SUSAN TOO: In harmony . . .

SUSAN: *Some*times in harmony . . .

SUSAN TOO: *(At window)* They're shooting baskets now.

SUSAN: Not the same thing as Frisbee.

SUSAN TOO: Ted looks more and more like his father. Remember how he liked to shoot baskets.

SUSAN: Remember how I kept telling him to grow up?

SUSAN TOO: "Take charge . . ."

SUSAN: "Be responsible . . ."

SUSAN TOO: "Be like me. Be like Sweet Sue."

SUSAN: No wonder he ran for the woods.

SUSAN TOO: *(Looking out)* They'll be hungry. I'll fix them something.

SUSAN: I already did.

SUSAN TOO: Then I'll get them a beer.

SUSAN: Leave them alone, why don't you.

SUSAN TOO: I can get my own son a beer, can't I? I can at least do that.

(She goes off. JAKE TOO *gets up and starts to follow)*

SUSAN: Hey, hey, hey! Where do you think you're going?

JAKE TOO: To get that beer.

SUSAN: But you're modeling for me.

JAKE TOO: No way.

SUSAN: But you—

JAKE TOO: It's just your fantasy, Mrs. Weatherill. I keep telling you, I'd never do that.

SUSAN: *(Calling after him)* But I want . . . I want to . . . (JAKE TOO *goes out as* JAKE *comes in.* SUSAN *turns to him)* I want to see you, Jake.

JAKE: That's what Ted said.

SUSAN: *(Beginning to set up her drawing implements)* Yes, I need your help. Ted very kindly gave me permission to ask you.

JAKE: Ask me what?

SUSAN: Ask your opinion, actually. Sit down please. It's a professional question. It seems that Hallmark is trying to expand its market. They want to go a little beyond hearts and flowers these days. They want to reach out more to your generation.

JAKE: Bridge the tragic gap?

SUSAN: Exactly. And apparently your generation likes to buy cards with a sense of humor. You like to express yourselves with some sort of joke.

JAKE: Oh, I don't know much about greeting cards.

SUSAN: Yes, you do. You're young. You're in tune with these things. I'm not. Actually, they rejected my last two ideas. They said Sweet Sue had fallen into a rut.

JAKE: Come on . . .

SUSAN: No, it's true. I'll admit it. I'll also admit the Dartmouth tuition has gone up another eight and a half percent. And my daughter on the West Coast is threatening to get married. So frankly, sir, I am somewhat on the line.

JAKE: *(Settling down)* O.K. Shoot.

SUSAN: Well, all right now. Lately I've been thinking about . . . life. *My* life, our life, in these United States. And I want to say something about it in my work. I mean, maybe I can do more this summer than simply draw trees. Maybe I can say something significant and still get paid for it, by those who send enough to care the very best.

JAKE: Good idea.

SUSAN: All right. So what I'm proposing to do is a series of cards—seven actually—based on the seven American holidays.

JAKE: Sounds good.

SUSAN: Now, wait. These cards would be organized around a specific theme.

JAKE: Go on.

SUSAN: I'm proposing to connect these seven American holidays with the Seven Deadly Sins.

JAKE: Sins?

SUSAN: Sins. Sweet Sue is turning to sin in her old age. What do you think?

JAKE: I don't know the Seven Deadly Sins, Mrs. Weatherill.

SUSAN: Well, you don't have to, really . . .

JAKE: I'm Presbyterian, not Catholic.

SUSAN: You're a human being, Jake. You have human . . . flaws, like everyone else.

JAKE: I'll say.

SUSAN: All right, then. Bear with me. I'll start with the three obvious ones. Christmas, for example, is Greed, or Covetousness. All that grabbing for presents. See?

JAKE: I'll buy that.

SUSAN: And Thanksgiving is Gluttony.

JAKE: That's for sure.

SUSAN: And Labor Day is Sloth, Jake. Laziness. Everyone sitting around.

JAKE: O.K.

SUSAN: Now we get trickier. What's the Fourth of July?

JAKE: Ummm . . .

SUSAN: Pride. False pride. Waving the flag.

JAKE: "What so proudly we hail . . ."

SUSAN: Exactly. All those stupid chest-thumping speeches . . .

JAKE: I'm with you.

SUSAN: Now, Easter. Or Passover. What do you think of there?

JAKE: I think of Fort Lauderdale . . .

SUSAN: Or churches . . .

JAKE: Or beaches . . .

SUSAN: Spring clothes . . .

JAKE: Beer . . . Burgers . . . Bodies . . .

SUSAN: Jake, pay attention. Easter is Envy.

JAKE: Right. I envy the guys who go to Fort Lauderdale.

SUSAN: There you are! And I envy the girls who go with them.

JAKE: O.K.

SUSAN: *(Crossing to the other side of him)* Let's try the next one the other way around. What goes with Anger?

JAKE: Anger?

SUSAN: What holiday?

JAKE: Let me think . . . Anger . . . Anger . . . Anger . . . *(He thinks)*

SUSAN: Jake, Anger is New Year's.

JAKE: *New* Year's? New Year's Day is Anger?

SUSAN: Anger that you drank too much. Anger that another wasted year has gone by. Anger that you're getting older by the minute.

JAKE: I don't look at New Year's that way, Mrs. Weatherill.

SUSAN: That's because you're young.

JAKE: I thought these cards were supposed to *be* for the young.

SUSAN: You're right. I'll have to rethink New Year's.

(She returns to her drawing board)

JAKE: I'm not much help to you on this, Mrs. Weatherill.

SUSAN: No, you are . . . you are. I'm learning a lot.

JAKE: I think I'm just messing you up.

SUSAN: No, really. There's one more, Jake. I've only given you six.

JAKE: I wasn't even counting.

SUSAN: I was. I saved it for last. What have we missed, Jake? Think. I'll bet we agree on this one . . . *(Pause. He thinks)* I'll give you a hint. It's not technically a holiday.

JAKE: Got it! Mother's Day.

SUSAN: *Mother's* Day?

JAKE: And the sin is Possessiveness.

SUSAN: I wasn't thinking of Mother's Day, Jake.

JAKE: You weren't?

SUSAN: No, I'm thinking of Valentine's Day.

JAKE: Valentine's Day? But what sin goes with Valentine's?

SUSAN: I thought Lust.

JAKE: Lust?

SUSAN: Lust, Lechery, Sex. Oh, I know they keep giving us hearts and flowers, but underneath it all is lust.

JAKE: Wow, Mrs. Weatherill.

SUSAN: That's what I think, anyway. That's what started me off on the whole series. That's what Freud thinks, too.

JAKE: I used to think that.

SUSAN: But you don't now?

JAKE: I'm trying not to.

SUSAN: Well, I'm trying to open a few doors for people. I think if we recognize these things, it's easier to deal with them. So do you like the idea?

JAKE: Of lust?

SUSAN: Of the whole thing. The Seven Deadly Sins.

JAKE: Sure.

SUSAN: You do?

JAKE: Sure.

SUSAN: Would you buy one of these cards?

JAKE: I might. Depending on what they looked like.

SUSAN: Of course. I understand that.

JAKE: I mean, what would you draw for Lust?

SUSAN: What would I draw?

JAKE: I mean, would you draw people . . . doing it?

SUSAN: I might. Discreetly, of course.

JAKE: Doing it *discreetly?*

SUSAN: Yes. You can suggest these things, Jake. There's a painting in the Louvre of this woman and this swan . . .

JAKE: I don't know, Mrs. Weatherill. I'm trying to get away from that stuff.

SUSAN: Now, wait a minute . . .

JAKE: *(Backing away)* I mean, I threw out all my copies of *Playboy* . . .

SUSAN: But I'm talking about . . .

JAKE: No, really. When I send Elaine a valentine, I think I'll just send her hearts and flowers.

(He goes out quickly up right)

SUSAN: *(Starting to follow him)* No, but wait—

(SUSAN TOO enters quickly from up left. She carries a checkbook and envelopes)

SUSAN TOO: Cool it.

SUSAN: But he made it sound all wrong.

SUSAN TOO: Didn't I tell you? It's dangerous to play with children. Now rise above it.

SUSAN: I'll work on New Year's.

SUSAN TOO: That's it. He goes his way, we go ours. Cool's the word.

(SUSAN *returns to her drawing table.* SUSAN TOO *pulls up a stool at the end as if it were a desk and starts making out checks.* JAKE TOO'*s voice is heard calling from offstage*)

JAKE TOO: *(Offstage)* Mrs. Weatherill!

SUSAN: Get that. Now that *is* childish.

SUSAN TOO: Instant gratification. We didn't hear it, did we?

SUSAN: No. We don't hear people who yell from way downstairs.

JAKE TOO: *(Offstage)* Mrs. Weatherill!

SUSAN TOO: *(Finally, quietly and calmly)* I'm up here, Jake.

SUSAN: That's it. Just . . . chill out.

SUSAN TOO: *(Making out another check)* Put our wagons in a circle.

(JAKE TOO *comes hurriedly into the room*)

JAKE TOO: Did I get a call yesterday?

SUSAN TOO: A call?

JAKE TOO: A telephone call. From Elaine.

SUSAN TOO: Elaine?

JAKE TOO: My girl.

SUSAN TOO: Ah, Miss Fudge Ripple.

SUSAN: *(To* SUSAN TOO*)* That's a good one. I like that.

SUSAN TOO: Thanks.

JAKE TOO: Did she call?

SUSAN TOO: I don't remember.

JAKE TOO: She said she called.

SUSAN TOO: Well, maybe she did.

JAKE TOO: She said she gave you a message. I was supposed to call her back.

SUSAN TOO: I remember now.

JAKE TOO: That was an important call, Mrs. Weatherill.

SUSAN TOO: I am not a social secretary, Jake.

SUSAN: *(To* SUSAN TOO*)* Good point.

SUSAN TOO: I think so.

JAKE TOO: Still . . .

SUSAN TOO: I do not sit by the telephone every minute of the day, taking cryptic messages. Though you may not believe it, Jake, I have other things on my mind. Such as these bills.

JAKE TOO: *(Starting out)* O.K., Mrs. Weatherill.

SUSAN TOO: Frankly, I thought it was your former little friend from the bar.

JAKE TOO: *(Exploding)* It was Elaine!

SUSAN TOO: *(Exploding)* Well, how am I supposed to know that? She doesn't say who she is! She doesn't announce herself.

SUSAN: *(To* SUSAN TOO*)* Go easy . . .

SUSAN TOO: I was always taught to say exactly who I was, first thing, on the telephone. It's known as manners.

SUSAN: Touché.

JAKE TOO: You don't like her, do you?

SUSAN TOO: I don't know her.

JAKE TOO: I can tell you don't like her.

SUSAN TOO: I've never met her, Jake. For some reason, you never bring her around.

JAKE TOO: She says you sound very cold on the telephone.

SUSAN TOO: That's her problem.

JAKE TOO: She gets nervous every time she calls.

SUSAN TOO: Well, then, maybe she shouldn't call quite so often.

JAKE TOO: We have to communicate, Mrs. Weatherill. We have to make plans.

SUSAN TOO: Then perhaps you could try to do that more on your own time.

JAKE TOO: *(Exasperatedly)* Oh Jesus. *(He walks out, up right)*

SUSAN: Well done.

SUSAN TOO: *(Returning to her checks)* Thank you.

SUSAN: Mayday! Mayday! Here he comes again.

SUSAN TOO: Your turn.

SUSAN: Gladly.

(JAKE *enters from down right)*

JAKE: What have you got against her, Mrs. Weatherill?

SUSAN: *(As she works)* Who?

JAKE: *Elaine.*

SUSAN: Not a thing.

JAKE: Tell me.

SUSAN: Jake, I've got to get this *done.*

JAKE: I want to know.

SUSAN: All right, Jake. Frankly, I think you can do better.

SUSAN TOO: That's good. That's constructive.

JAKE: What does that mean?

SUSAN: Well, it might mean that she sounds a little, well, cheap.

JAKE: She goes to *Skid*more College!

SUSAN: I can't help that, Jake. All I know is there's some strange, breathy little voice on the other end of the telephone which I keep thinking is that bar girl you wanted to get rid of.

SUSAN TOO: *(Looking up from her checks)* Don't overdo it.

SUSAN: Sorry.

JAKE: They are not the same type at all!

SUSAN: Apparently not.

JAKE: This girl is very important to me!

SUSAN: Apparently.

JAKE: I'm becoming very involved with her, Mrs. Weatherill!

SUSAN: Well, you see, I didn't know. You didn't tell me. I had no idea your entire future depended on that teeny, tiny little voice.

JAKE: Oh Jesus!

(He storms out right)

SUSAN: *(Getting up to follow him)* I'm sorry, Jake, that was very cruel . . .

SUSAN TOO: *(Holding her back)* Hold on . . . Calm down . . .

(JAKE TOO *comes in quickly from up right)*

JAKE TOO: *(Angrily)* She didn't call *today,* did she?

SUSAN TOO: Are you speaking to me in that tone of voice?

JAKE TOO: *(Sarcastically)* A thousand pardons, Mrs. Weatherill, ma'am, but by any chance did Elaine call today?

SUSAN TOO: Today?

JAKE TOO: While I was at work.

SUSAN TOO: I don't know.

JAKE TOO: You don't *know?*

SUSAN TOO: I had to go out, Jake. I had to buy food. I had to take things to the cleaners.

SUSAN: I had to get the toaster fixed. For the second time this summer.

(JAKE *enters from down right)*

JAKE: Didn't you put the answering machine on?

SUSAN: I forgot.

JAKE: I can't *believe* you didn't put the machine on.

SUSAN: I for*got*.

JAKE: Shit.

SUSAN: I do not appreciate that language, Jake.

JAKE: She's been probably trying to get me all afternoon!

(He grabs the telephone, dials, his back to the audience)

JAKE TOO: Shit, shit, shit! *(He starts to leave, then turns back)* We have to talk about this.

SUSAN TOO: What else is there to say?

JAKE TOO: We used to get along so well.

SUSAN: I just don't like it, Jake.

JAKE TOO: O.K., I'll tell her not to call here any more.

SUSAN TOO: That would be helpful.

JAKE TOO: And I'll try to stay out of your way.

SUSAN: That might make sense.

JAKE TOO: I dunno. You and I had such a good thing going. Pisses me off somehow. *(He goes out, up right)*

SUSAN: Oh God. *(Starts to follow him)*

SUSAN TOO: *(Restraining her)* Leave it alone.

SUSAN: But he—

SUSAN TOO: Leave it *alone!* Just . . . go about your business . . . Just keep it . . . business as usual.

JAKE: *(On telephone)* O.K. . . . See you later . . . You, too. *(Hangs up, turns to* SUSAN*)* She got home all right.

SUSAN: Good. I'm glad. (JAKE *starts out)* Jake . . . *(He stops)* I'm sorry if I've been disagreeable. I've been a little tired lately.

JAKE: O.K., forget it, Mrs. Weatherill.

SUSAN: All this is very new to me. Having you here all summer. Nancy coming and going, a lot of doors opening and closing all night long. I've been having trouble sleeping.

JAKE: I didn't know that, Mrs. Weatherill.

SUSAN: Oh, I'm all right. I'm fine. I'll survive.

SUSAN TOO: I won't hurl myself under a train like Anna Karenina.

SUSAN: Actually, I had a doctor's appointment. That's really why I went out. He gave me some new pills. Pills continue to be the solution for Sweet Sue. *(She sits down behind the table)*

JAKE: We'll be quieter, Mrs. Weatherill. I swear.

SUSAN: No, no. It's just that I'm a silly old-fashioned suburban lady without a husband and I don't always . . . I'm not used to . . . Oh dear. *(She tries not to cry)*

JAKE: *(Going to her, standing behind her)* Oh, hey, Mrs. Weatherill.

(He puts his hands on her shoulders, she puts her face against his hand. There is a moment. SUSAN TOO *shakes her head disapprovingly)*

SUSAN TOO: This Elaine. Will you be seeing her tonight?

JAKE: Sure.

SUSAN TOO: Tell you what. Why don't you bring her around?

JAKE: Around?

SUSAN TOO: So I can meet her, Jake. That way, the next time she calls, I'll be able to connect a face with a voice.

SUSAN: I won't feel quite so much like an answering service.

SUSAN TOO: Maybe I've got her all wrong.

SUSAN: I'd love to meet her, Jake.

SUSAN TOO: So bring her around.

JAKE: I don't want to, Mrs. Weatherill.

SUSAN TOO: Why not?

JAKE: I can't put you and Elaine together.

SUSAN TOO: Are you ashamed of her?

JAKE: NO! Not ashamed . . . ! She's the greatest girl I've ever met!

(He goes off, up right)

(Pause)

SUSAN: *(As they clean up)* Well. She can't be *that* great. Ted says she's quite short, actually . . . tiny . . . minuscule.

SUSAN TOO: Compared to Nancy.

(Pause)

Who seems gigantic.

(Pause)

I thought we did very well just then.

SUSAN: Are you losing your marbles?

SUSAN TOO: I thought we did very well. For the most part.

SUSAN: Was that a crack?

SUSAN TOO: Not really.

SUSAN: That was a crack, wasn't it?

SUSAN TOO: I just don't believe in going to pieces.

SUSAN: Oh God.

SUSAN TOO: I suppose you did it so he'd have to touch you.

SUSAN: *What?* As if I weren't onto all your phoney "bring her around" stuff.

SUSAN TOO: I simply wanted to bring her into the picture.

SUSAN: You simply wanted to throttle her with your bare hands.

SUSAN TOO: I will not dignify that remark with an answer.

(JAKE TOO *enters from up right and throws himself discouragedly onto the daybed*)

SUSAN: We're not in sync any more, are we?

SUSAN TOO: Not much. No.

SUSAN: I suppose the psychiatrists have a word for it.

SUSAN TOO: Do you think we should see one?

SUSAN: I don't know. He'd probably charge us double.

SUSAN TOO: I know what he'd say anyway.

SUSAN: What?

SUSAN TOO: He'd say we're side-stepping our own feelings. He'd say we're just tossing the ball back and forth between ourselves. He'd say we've done this all summer.

SUSAN: He'd say we've done this all our lives.

SUSAN TOO: Yes . . .

SUSAN: Well, it's not working. I don't know who I am any more.

SUSAN TOO: I know one thing.

SUSAN: What's that?

SUSAN TOO: I think it's time I got married. *(She goes off, up left)*

SUSAN: *(Following her)* What? When? Who to?

(She goes off, as JAKE TOO *turns on the radio by his bed. Rock music, the Talking Heads, comes up loudly. He gets up and dances wildly to it, then* SUSAN TOO *appears, as if at the door)*

SUSAN TOO: Jake? May I come in?

JAKE TOO: *(Embarrassed, throwing himself on the bed)* It's your studio.

(She comes in hesitantly)

SUSAN TOO: May I turn off the music?

JAKE TOO: It's your radio, too.

(She turns off the radio; pause)

SUSAN TOO: Jake, what would you say if I got married?

JAKE TOO: What would Ted say, you mean?

SUSAN TOO: I know what Ted would say. Ted would say fine.

JAKE TOO: *(Sitting up)* To this guy on Martha's Vineyard?

SUSAN TOO: Harvey Satterfield.

JAKE TOO: You mean he's asked you?

SUSAN TOO: Many times.

JAKE TOO: How come you haven't done it?

SUSAN TOO: I didn't think I loved him.

JAKE TOO: But you do now?

SUSAN TOO: I like him very much. We get along extremely well. If I put one of those ads in *The New York Review of Books* describing exactly what I wanted as a companion, Harvey would fill the bill perfectly.

JAKE TOO: Oh yeah?

SUSAN TOO: *(Coming downstage)* I just called him and asked if I could come visit again and he suggested I stay for a whole week, which means he'll ask me to marry him. If he doesn't, goddammit, I'll ask *him.*

JAKE TOO: *(Getting up)* Go for it, Mrs. Weatherill.

SUSAN TOO: Think I should?

JAKE TOO: Sure. Go ahead. Make your move.

SUSAN TOO: Maybe you just want to get rid of me, so you can have a huge orgy all over the house.

JAKE TOO: Maybe you'll have your own up there, Mrs. Weatherill.

(Pause)

SUSAN TOO: I'm not sure I love him, Jake.

JAKE TOO: Do you love anyone else?

SUSAN TOO: No. Of course not . . . No.

JAKE TOO: Then maybe you love him and don't know it.

SUSAN TOO: I doubt that, Jake.

JAKE TOO: It can happen, you know. You can be passionate about a person and not even realize it.

SUSAN TOO: Oh yes?

JAKE TOO: It happened to me. This summer.

SUSAN TOO: With Elaine?

JAKE TOO: With you.

SUSAN TOO: With *me?*

JAKE TOO: With you, Mrs. Weatherill.

SUSAN TOO: How with me?

JAKE TOO: Don't you remember how I got hung up on you the first part of the summer? Don't you remember?

SUSAN TOO: Oh yes.

JAKE TOO: You called it infatuation, but it was more than that. I'd never met a woman like you before. Ever. So intelligent. So complicated. So on top of things.

SUSAN TOO: Oh, that's just because I'm older.

JAKE TOO: You changed my life, Mrs. Weatherill.

SUSAN TOO: How did I do that?

JAKE TOO: Remember I told you I thought of women as sex objects . . .

SUSAN TOO: I remember . . .

JAKE TOO: How I'd be trying to make conversation and take them seriously, when all I really wanted to do was grab their tits.

SUSAN TOO: *(Ironically)* I believe I recall some such concern.

JAKE TOO: Well, that was my problem. I didn't know how to treat a woman. Until I met you.

(JAKE *enters quickly from up right*)

JAKE: And there's one other thing I want to say.

SUSAN TOO: What?

JAKE: For a while I even thought I might be gay.

SUSAN TOO: Gay?

JAKE TOO: Oh, not *gay,* really . . .

JAKE: Or something like it. Because I couldn't deal with women in a real way. I used to go to church every Sunday, and pray like crazy: "Please, God. Straighten me out with women. Don't let me go gay. Don't make me spend my life selling antiques."

SUSAN TOO: Oh, I'm sure every young boy . . .

JAKE: No, it continued. Even at Dartmouth, I thought I might be gay.

JAKE TOO: Not gay, exactly. Jesus, I went out with girls, made out with them, all that.

JAKE: But I wasn't really connecting with them. I was just using them, going through the motions.

JAKE TOO: I mean, I *liked* them.

JAKE: I just liked the guys more.

JAKE TOO: In certain *areas.* Hanging out. Drinking beer. Skiing. Playing football or Frisbee . . .

JAKE: But whenever girls got involved, they always seemed to mess it up.

JAKE TOO: In those areas, at least.

JAKE: So I secretly thought I might be this closet gay.

JAKE TOO: Well maybe not *gay* . . .

JAKE: Yes, *gay,* actually. Even at Dartmouth, that's what I thought I might be.

SUSAN TOO: *(Sitting on the stool, downstage)* What made you decide to focus your orientation?

JAKE TOO: You.

SUSAN TOO: Me?

JAKE: You, Mrs. Weatherill.

SUSAN TOO: Good Lord, what did I do?

JAKE TOO: You took me out to dinner.

JAKE: Up at Dartmouth. On Parents' Day.

JAKE TOO: You took me to the Surf and Turf.

JAKE: You talked to me . . .

JAKE TOO: You listened . . . You took me seriously . . .

SUSAN TOO: Oh well. Big deal.

JAKE: No, I'm serious, Mrs. Weatherill. That's what did it.

JAKE TOO: I thought you were awesome.

JAKE: That's why I came here this summer.

JAKE TOO: I thought I wanted to meet a girl.

JAKE: But now I know it was really just to meet you.

SUSAN TOO: How do you do.

JAKE: I'm serious, Mrs. Weatherill.

JAKE TOO: I'm really serious.

(Pause)

SUSAN TOO: So you came.

JAKE TOO: Right. And you didn't treat me like a kid or student . . .

JAKE: At least, most of the time you didn't . . .

JAKE TOO: I mean, there you were, this gorgeous woman . . .

JAKE: Who was my roommate's *mother,* for God's sake . . .

JAKE TOO: But gorgeous . . .

JAKE: But a mature woman . . .

JAKE TOO: Not old, though. I don't mean old . . .

JAKE: Just sort of mellow, actually. Just sort of ripe . . .

JAKE TOO: But gorgeous. Really gorgeous, sometimes . . .

JAKE: So here was this gorgeous woman, coming on to me . . .

JAKE TOO: Not coming on. I don't mean coming on . . .

JAKE: Treating me like you *could* come on . . .

JAKE TOO: Treating me like a man.

JAKE: That's it. Treating me like a man. That's what happened here this summer, Mrs. Weatherill.

JAKE TOO: I fell in love with you this summer, Mrs. Weatherill.

JAKE: Because you treated me like a man.

(Pause)

SUSAN TOO: Well, you are. You are a man. It's not too tough to treat you like one.

JAKE: *(Getting his jacket from behind the loveseat)* Well, all I know, Mrs. Weatherill, is that if it hadn't been for you, I'd never have fallen in love with Elaine.

SUSAN TOO: I see.

JAKE: And because of you, I've also decided to get back into the pre-med program at Dartmouth. I think I can be a decent doctor now, rather than just a rapist in residence. *(With a glance at JAKE TOO)*

SUSAN TOO: That's fine, Jake.

JAKE: God, this is incredible! Here I am, making an important career choice and developing an intense new personal relationship! All because of you, Mrs. Weatherill! You've saved my life. It's as simple as that. *(He goes out, right)*

JAKE TOO: *(Looking after him)* Sometimes I think that's all a crock.

SUSAN TOO: A crock?

JAKE TOO: About me and Elaine. Sometimes I think I'm just glomming onto her so I don't glom onto you.

SUSAN TOO: Oh, Jake . . .

(She stands up)

JAKE TOO: I mean it. That's why I keep you apart. I'm scared if I put you two together, you'd blow her away.

SUSAN TOO: Oh heavens . . .

JAKE TOO: Yeah, well, at least you started the ball rolling in the right direction, Mrs. Weatherill.

SUSAN TOO: Toward Elaine.

JAKE TOO: Right. And the same might be true for you and that guy on the Vineyard.

SUSAN TOO: Harvey Satterfield.

JAKE TOO: Right. I mean, you might love him now.

SUSAN TOO: You think so?

JAKE TOO: You might.

SUSAN TOO: And you think you started that ball rolling for me, Jake?

JAKE TOO: Maybe. I could have. I hope I did.

SUSAN TOO: Well. Let's hope you're right.

JAKE TOO: You think you'll marry him?

SUSAN TOO: I think I'd better.

JAKE TOO: Mrs. Weatherill . . .

SUSAN TOO: Yes?

JAKE TOO: May I kiss the bride?

(Pause)

SUSAN TOO: All right. *(She stands stiffly. He approaches her. She presents her cheek. He kisses it. She almost holds him, but doesn't finally)* You'll be late for Elaine.

JAKE TOO: Right. *(He starts off quickly up right. She stands in the same spot, enthralled. He stops upstage, comes back down immediately)* Mrs. Weatherill . . .

SUSAN TOO: *Don't,* don't, don't say anything more!

JAKE TOO: *(Whispering)* Ted's down there. His door is open. I think he heard what we said.

SUSAN TOO: I'd better—talk to him.

(She goes off quickly down right. JAKE TOO *follows as* JAKE *enters from up right holding a bloody handkerchief to his nose.* SUSAN *comes on immediately behind him)*

SUSAN: What happened?

JAKE: I guess he landed one.

SUSAN: I thought you were taking a good long walk together.

JAKE: We got as far as the end of the driveway.

SUSAN: *(Getting a cloth)* Let me help.

JAKE: Help Ted. He looks worse than I do.

SUSAN: Ted's got Nancy.

JAKE: He asked what the story was.

SUSAN: I *told* him. I said you may have had a little crush on me.

JAKE: I said I'd been in love with you since Dartmouth.

SUSAN: Oh, Jake . . .

JAKE: I said it was over now. Or I hoped it was.

SUSAN: Oh gosh.

JAKE: I'm glad I told him. I felt good telling him.

SUSAN: Oh boy, oh boy.

JAKE: He wanted to know if it was true for you.

SUSAN: What did you say?

JAKE: I said, "NO! No way!" I said you might be just a little infatuated. That's when he hit me. And I hit him back.

SUSAN: I'll talk to him again.

JAKE: He told me to shove off.

(He gets his backpack out from under the daybed)

SUSAN: No. No. Now wait. Please. I know I can clear this up.

(SUSAN goes out down right, as SUSAN TOO enters up right)

SUSAN TOO: Ted says he's leaving, too.

JAKE: Why?

SUSAN TOO: He wants to visit his father.

JAKE: Oh yeah?

SUSAN TOO: With Nancy.

JAKE: No kidding.

SUSAN TOO: He wants to *stay* there, Jake. He says he's sold his father short.

JAKE: He'll be back.

SUSAN TOO: Who knows? Maybe not.

JAKE: Come on, Mrs. Weatherill.

SUSAN TOO: I've lost him, Jake. I think I've lost him.

JAKE: Oh no.

SUSAN TOO: *(Crossing to drawing table)* I've lost my job, too. Did you know that? Hallmark called last week and canceled our arrangement.

JAKE: Those bastards.

SUSAN TOO: All because of my Seven Deadly Sins.

JAKE: I liked that idea.

SUSAN TOO: It was dumb, Jake. A dumb idea. How could I be so dumb?

(SUSAN *comes back in from right)*

SUSAN: I just called up Harvey at the Vineyard and told him I couldn't come. He offered me a rain check. Tomorrow, next week, any time. But I won't go. *(She sits on the loveseat)*

JAKE: You should, Mrs. Weatherill.

SUSAN: I can't, Jake. It's not a solution.

(JAKE TOO *comes on from right; He carries a check)*

JAKE TOO: The "boss" just paid me off.

(He hands it to JAKE*)*

SUSAN: At least you're speaking.

JAKE TOO: Oh sure. Nancy even made us shake hands.

JAKE: We won't room together next fall, we agreed to that.

JAKE TOO: But at least we exchanged words.

SUSAN: *(Getting up)* Oh, then maybe we're all jumping the gun.

SUSAN TOO: *(Coming around the table)* Maybe nobody should leave until we talk.

SUSAN: Talk things out.

SUSAN TOO: Yes. Sit down. Have a beer. Say good-bye in a civilized fashion, which is what I've wanted all along.

SUSAN: Get Ted and we'll talk.

JAKE TOO: He's gone, Mrs. Weatherill.

SUSAN: Gone?

SUSAN TOO: Without saying good-bye?

JAKE TOO: He'll call from his dad's. He said he had to get out of this house.

JAKE: *(Taking up his backpack)* He told me to go too.

JAKE TOO: That was part of the deal. *(He goes to dial the telephone)*

SUSAN: *(To* JAKE*)* But what about your job?

SUSAN TOO: You have an obligation.

SUSAN: The Millworths' house is only half done.

SUSAN TOO: You can't just walk away from a half-painted house.

JAKE: Bobby Peretti's taking over.

SUSAN: But you need the money! For college!

JAKE: I'll survive.

JAKE TOO: *(On telephone)* May I speak to Elaine, please?

SUSAN: At least let me drive you to the bus.

JAKE: That's O.K.

SUSAN: I want to do it.

JAKE: *(Starting out up right)* I'm not going to the bus.

JAKE TOO: *(On telephone)* Hi. *(Turns upstage)*

SUSAN: Are you going over to her house?

JAKE: I think so.

SUSAN: You mean, stay there?

JAKE: I think.

SUSAN: You mean you'll hang around there the rest of the summer?

JAKE: Maybe I can work for Bobby Peretti.

(JAKE TOO continues to talk on the telephone)

SUSAN TOO: Well. Everyone seems to have solved their problems very nicely this summer.

SUSAN: You . . . Ted . . . Nancy . . . Elaine . . .

(They begin to swirl around JAKE)

SUSAN TOO: Bobby Peretti . . .

SUSAN: Even Ted's father seems to have come out ahead.

SUSAN TOO: Everyone gets a happy ending.

SUSAN: Except me.

JAKE: Oh, Mrs. Weatherill . . .

SUSAN: I'm kind of left holding the bag.

SUSAN TOO: "Sweet Sue . . . Just you . . ."

JAKE: Oh hey . . .

SUSAN: I'm left with a broken washing machine, for example . . .

JAKE: I didn't break the—

SUSAN: You overloaded it. Twice.

SUSAN TOO: And you spilled beer on the carpet.

JAKE: That wasn't me.

SUSAN TOO: There is a huge spot!

JAKE: I'll pay for it, right now.

SUSAN: It's not the money, Jake.

SUSAN TOO: It's not the money at all.

SUSAN: It's just that I'm beginning to feel a little exploited around
here . . .

SUSAN TOO: I mean, I devoted my summer to you . . .

SUSAN: Gave you my work space . . .

SUSAN TOO: Gave you everything you wanted . . .

SUSAN: Free room. Free board. Free love . . .

JAKE: Oh now, come on . . .

SUSAN: And what happens? I lose my job, I lose my son, I'm left here stranded . . .

JAKE TOO: *(Into telephone)* Call you back. There's trouble here . . . *(He hangs up)*

SUSAN TOO: I mean, what am I? A doormat? A meal ticket? A cleaning woman?

SUSAN: I am an artist! That's what I am! And I've wasted my valuable summer because of you!

SUSAN TOO: And when I asked you to do me one favor . . .

SUSAN: One small favor . . .

SUSAN TOO: One easy thing, which might help me in my work . . .

SUSAN: Might help me develop and stretch and grow beyond this grim suburban prison I've been locked in half my life . . .

JAKE TOO: O.K., O.K. . . .

SUSAN TOO: And for which I offered to pay twenty-five dollars an hour . . .

JAKE: *(Exploding) All right, Mrs. Weatherill! (He begins ripping off his clothes)* I'll model for you! I'll model for you right now! *(He throws off his clothes)* Here I am! Is this what you want? Want to see me naked, Mrs. Weatherill? Here I am! Draw me! *(He sits on the stool defiantly, facing her, echoing the same position we saw at the start of both acts)* Go on, Susan! Draw me! Get me down pat!

(SUSAN *hides her face in her hands.* SUSAN TOO *turns away)*

SUSAN: Oh, Jake.

JAKE TOO: Oh Jesus . . . I guess I kind of went overboard, didn't I? I guess I kind of freaked out. *(He hurries down and begins to pick up the scattered clothes, handing them to* JAKE*)* Here's your pants. Here's your shirt . . . Here's your shoes. *(To* SUSAN*)* I apologize, Mrs. Weatherill. I want to apologize for my rude behavior.

(He helps JAKE *get dressed, then kneels beside him)*

SUSAN TOO: I love you, Jake.

JAKE TOO: Mrs. Weatherill . . .

SUSAN: No, I do. I love you.

JAKE TOO: Hey, Mrs. Weatherill . . .

SUSAN: No, I do. I think about you all the time.

SUSAN TOO: I dream about you.

SUSAN: You're on my mind every minute of the day.

JAKE TOO: It's not love, Mrs. Weatherill. It's just infatuation.

SUSAN: Oh, is that it? Infatuation . . .

SUSAN TOO: Not love?

SUSAN: It's not love when I rush to the window to get one last glimpse of you as you leave in the morning. It's not love when I'm waiting at that same window from four-thirty on, peering down the street, watching for you to come home. It's not love when I hear your voice in the house and I drop whatever I'm doing to come down and offer you food, beer, anything, so I have an excuse to be in the same room with you. Or when I ask you the silliest questions . . .

SUSAN TOO: How was your day?

SUSAN: What color paint did you use?

SUSAN TOO: How are the Red Sox doing?

SUSAN: Anything, so we can talk, so I can talk, so I can hold you here a little longer . . .

JAKE: Mrs. Weatherill . . .

SUSAN: No, please. Don't stop me now. It took me so long to get started . . .

SUSAN TOO: Besides, I'm learning something . . .

SUSAN: I'm learning from the younger generation . . .

SUSAN TOO: I'm learning what love is not.

SUSAN: So it's not love, is it, when all my conversations with my son, my own son, my only son, are always about you.

SUSAN TOO: "Tell me about him, Ted. Tell me about his family."

SUSAN: "What's he like at school?"

SUSAN TOO: "Does he have many friends?"

SUSAN: "Does he have many girls?"

SUSAN TOO: "Tell me more, tell me all, tell me anything."

SUSAN: But that's not love.

SUSAN TOO: Oh well, then, Jake, if it's not love, then after all these years, I don't know what love is. Because this is like nothing I've ever felt before, ever. Not with my poor, lost husband during those sweet first years of our marriage. Not with Bud Wainwright. Not with Harvey Satterfield on the Vineyard this summer. Well, all I know is I'm sick, Jake, I'm falling apart, I'm dying, even though you assure me it's not love.

(Pause)

JAKE: *(Quietly, sincerely, to* SUSAN*)* Do you want me to sleep with you?

JAKE TOO: *(To* SUSAN TOO*)* Do you want me to sleep with you, Susan?

(Pause)

SUSAN TOO: No thank you, Jake.

SUSAN: Thank you . . .

SUSAN TOO: But no.

(The sound of a car horn is heard)

JAKE TOO: There's my ride.

SUSAN TOO: Elaine.

JAKE TOO: Right.

SUSAN TOO: You'd better go.

JAKE TOO: O.K.

(Both JAKES *get up.* JAKE *hugs* SUSAN, JAKE TOO *looks at* SUSAN TOO*)*

JAKE: Think of the alternative, Mrs. Weatherill.

JAKE TOO: I mean, where would it lead?

JAKE: Where would it lead if we got together?

JAKE TOO: Imagine, you and me . . .

JAKE: You and me . . . in the future?

SUSAN: Just go, Jake. Please.

SUSAN TOO: Just go.

(Both JAKES *exit up right,* JAKE *grabbing the backpack on the way)*

(Pause)

SUSAN: What do I do now?

SUSAN TOO: Suppose you went after him?

SUSAN: Dreaming again.

SUSAN TOO: Suppose you did. Suppose you bridged that tragic gap? (SUSAN *looks at her, then exits quickly right.* SUSAN TOO *speaks as if to herself)* She dashed down the stairs and caught up to him in the front hall. They fell into a mad embrace. They forgot Ted, forgot Elaine, forgot everything but themselves. They made love all day long in her double bed. They met again three times during the rest of the summer: New York, for a delicious weekend; that secluded inn on the water, near New London, for an afternoon; Aunt Esther's apartment in Boston over Labor Day. It was there they decided not to see each other any more. She gave him her drawing of an apple. They took a walk on Newbury Street. She got cold. He bought her a plum-colored sweater to keep her warm.

(SUSAN comes back in from the right, wearing a plum-colored sweater)

SUSAN: He's gone.

SUSAN TOO: Yes.

SUSAN: I offered him a beer. I said we should at least sit down and share a beer. But he had to go.

(SUSAN TOO clears the sheets from the rumpled daybed)

SUSAN TOO: Yes.

SUSAN: I said, "Hey look, we should talk. I'm not that old. You're not that young. It doesn't always have to be so *tragic.*" But he left.

SUSAN TOO: *(Goes to window, looks out)* He's gone?

SUSAN: Yes.

SUSAN TOO: Forever?

SUSAN: Yes.

(SUSAN TOO *gets the sketch pad, sits centerstage, and idly begins to sketch the empty stool where* JAKE *sat)*

SUSAN TOO: At least I have this.

SUSAN: *(Taking a bottle of pills from her skirt pocket, looking at them)* Or these.

SUSAN TOO: Don't be silly.

SUSAN: I don't think I can—

SUSAN TOO: *(Singing insistently)* "Every star above . . . Knows the one I love . . ."

SUSAN: How can you work at a time like this? *(Crossing behind her looking over her shoulder)* It's not bad, I'll say that.

SUSAN TOO: Thanks.

SUSAN: Quite good, actually.

SUSAN TOO: Thank you very much.

SUSAN: *(Putting the pills on the drawing table, taking up a pencil)* Doesn't look like him, though.

SUSAN TOO: Better if it doesn't.

SUSAN: *(Leaning over, adding a flourish)* What if I do this?

SUSAN TOO: Good. Excellent.

(They work together on the drawing)

BOTH: *(Singing)* "No one else it seems . . . Ever shares my dreams . . ." *(They try harmony)* "And without you, dear . . . I don't know what I'd do . . ."

SUSAN: Do you realize this is the first time in my life I've ever drawn a sex organ on anything?

SUSAN TOO: Make it bigger.

SUSAN: Know something?

SUSAN TOO: What?

SUSAN: This is good.

SUSAN TOO: Oh yes?

SUSAN: This is very good.

SUSAN TOO: You think so?

(She gets up quickly, leans the drawing against the stool downstage; They both stand back and look at it)

SUSAN: This is the best thing I've done.

SUSAN TOO: I think so, too.

(They stand admiring their work, arm in arm, as the lights fade on them and the recording of "Sweet Sue" comes up)

THE END